TOO CLEVER
FOR OUR OWN GOOD

Hidden Facets of Human Evolution

Kaoru Yamamoto

University Press of America,® Inc.
Lanham · Boulder · New York · Toronto · Plymouth, UK

Copyright © 2007 by
University Press of America,® Inc.
4501 Forbes Boulevard
Suite 200
Lanham, Maryland 20706
UPA Acquisitions Department (301) 459-3366

Estover Road
Plymouth PL6 7PY
United Kingdom

Library of Congress Control Number: 2007922675
ISBN-13: 978-0-7618-3761-9 (clothbound : alk. paper)
ISBN-10: 0-7618-3761-2 (clothbound : alk. paper)
ISBN-13: 978-0-7618-3762-6 (paperback : alk. paper)
ISBN-10: 0-7618-3762-0 (paperback : alk. paper)

Dedication

To all the significant members of the Moore family —

Carol-Lynne, Keita Carey, Kiyomi Lynne,

Granddad Robb, Grandmom Martha-Lynne,

Uncle Paul, and Aunt Ann.

Table of Contents

List of Tables

List of Figures

Prologue

Homo sapiens is a peculiar creature in many ways. Only our unavoidable familiarity keeps us from finding ourselves strange and perhaps even a little scary! Even so, we sometimes find our own kind incomprehensible and almost alien. In the face of senseless acts of callousness, cruelty, and destructiveness, for instance, we stand speechless and feel powerless. Likewise, in witnessing unbelievable deeds of prowess, selflessness, or heroism, some disbelief is mixed in with our admiration. Meanwhile, one of the notable singularities is that, whereas "every animal leaves traces of what it was; man alone leaves traces of what he created."[1] We usually learn what a particular animal must have been from its corporal remains, but our speculations about our own species are much richer because of the frequent availability of the artifacts built and left behind.

In the continuity carried through such human creations, "the past is ... the live, active force that sustains our today.... The past is not yonder, at the date when it happened, but here, in me."[2] From the megalithic monuments on windswept fields to the galleons buried deep in sea bottoms, from the rock paintings in dark caves to the songs, dances, and folk tales kept alive across generations, the embodiments of past imaginations carry the unique legacy of humans into the present and on to the future.

"Through the development of [all] this technology—through the use of their hands and their minds—they created an existence that spared their bodies."[3] Technics was born—"that part of human activity wherein ... man controls and directs the forces of nature for his own purposes."[4] Understandably, "like children or savages, we have delighted ourselves with technics. We have thought they alone might free us."[5] Even human evolution has changed its character with the enhancement of power through technics.

This phenomenon has undoubtedly been a great boon in many ways for the whole species. Yet, the very power that so enables us can also ensnare and enfeeble us. An apt reminder of this fact was already given by the Renaissance humanist, Giovanni Pico della Mirandola (1463-1494), in the imaginary admonition given by God to Adam, who was His creation unlike any other. It includes the following lines.

> Thou, constrained by no limits ... shalt ordain for thyself the limits of thy nature.... As the maker and molder of thyself in whatever shape thou shalt prefer, thou shalt have the power to degenerate into lower forms of life, which are brutish. Thou shalt have the power, out of thy soul and judgment, to be reborn into the higher form, which are divine.[6]

At every stage in their development, that choice faces the humans. To explore the nature of that potentially constructive, as well as destructive, power closely, this book traces our past and considers some of the ramifications for our present and future.

Notes

1. Bronowski, 1981, 27.
2. Ortega y Gasset, 1962, 223.
3. Gaylin, 1991, 163.
4. Mumford, 1952, 15.
5. Eiseley, 1980, 146.
6. Mumford, 1967, 47.

Chapter 1. The Long March

Peculiarity is obviously not a human monopoly. Every creature looks peculiar to any others, and is peculiar in its own way. This feature we share with all other life forms. As Loren Eiseley noted half a century ago,

> Every creature alive is the product of a unique history. The statistical probability of its precise reduplication on another planet is so small as to be meaningless. Life, even cellular life, may exist out yonder in the dark. But high and low in nature, it will not wear the shape of man. That shape is the evolutionary product of a strange, long wandering through the attics of the forest roof, and so great are the chances of failure, that nothing precisely and identically human is likely ever to come that way again.[1]

Beyond this awareness itself, what other characteristics make our own peculiarities so peculiar? In pondering this question, most observers point to two factors that together lead to the unique human configuration. These are (a) the creature's bipedality and (b) its brain mass.[2] But, first, let us review our long past.

The Trail of the Creature

Homo sapiens is the only surviving species in the genus, *Homo*, that dates back 2-3 million years. Taxonomically, the *Homo* belongs to the family, *Hominidae*, which is in turn a part of the order of *Primates*, or all placental mammals including lemurs, lorises, monkeys, apes, and man. The exact lineage of *Homo sapiens* is apparently still difficult to establish, but "the transition to walking upright seems to have happened around four million years ago with *Ramidus*," whose 4½-million-year-old fossil was discovered in Ethiopia in 1993. This creature is now regarded as "intermediate ... between the fully upright walkers that existed a million years later and the apes of six million years earlier."[3] As a hominid, i.e., an ancient ape-like human ancestor, *Australopithecus ramidus* was found to predate *Australopithecus afarensis* (3 to 4 million years back) or *Australopithecus africanus* (2 to 3 million years ago).[4] An even more recent discovery in Chad of *Sahelanthropus tchadensis* appears to push the earliest known age of hominid back to 6 to 7 million years ago.[5]

In any case, the speculation is that recurrent droughts between 5 and 8 million years back so degraded the ancestral forest habitat in tropical Africa as to force some of the arboreal animals to leave the trees behind to seek a new life in the savannas. The start of anatomical modifications, which were needed for the upright posture and fast terrestrial locomotion in the more exposed surroundings, was already in evidence in the remains of *Australopithecus* (meaning the "southern ape"). The foot bones, ankle joints, and hips were in the process of adjustment to bear the body weight on the ground, while the hands, now released from their supportive functions, were becoming more flexible for gathering, carrying, and manipulating things.

By 2½ million years ago, *Homo habilis* (the "handyman" of eastern and southern Africa) or *Homo ergaster* (the "action man" of eastern Africa) was habitually bipedal, using simple stone tools, and omnivorous.. By that time, the hominid brain size had doubled. [It would double again in the course of the next 2 million years.] The subsequent *Homo erectus* (the "erect man"), ½ to 2 million years back, augmented life by making and using fire and organizing social enterprises like group hunt. It is also believed that this was the species of great migrants out of Africa,[6] leaving fossils in such far away places like Java *(Homo erectus erectus)* and China *(Homo erectus pekinensis)*.

According to Jonathan Kingdon,[7] perhaps between 600,000 to 200,000 years ago, creatures now classified as *Homo sapiens* finally arrived on the scene, some of them even overlapping with the last of the *Erectus* for quite a while. Though their own source is unclear, the earliest *Homo sapiens heidelbergensis* (the Heidelberg man) of Africa and Europe is believed to have given rise to at least three regional populations, namely, *Homo sapiens neanderthalensis* (the Neanderthals) in Europe, *Homo sapiens mapaensis* (the Mapas) in East Asia, and *Homo sapiens sapiens* (the Moderns) in Africa. The latest discovery of *Homo sapiens idaltu* gives evidence of a 160,000-year-old subspecies of the Moderns in Ethiopia.[8]

By the time of the glacial period of 150,000 to 130,000 years ago, the Mapas may have been gone, but the Modern humans spread beyond Africa to survive the three frigid waves that came approximately 20,000 years apart from 100,000 years back.[9] By the latest severe Ice Age that began about 30,000 years ago, the little understood Neanderthals were extinct after having co-inhabited the earth for nearly 10,000 years with the Moderns (e.g., Cro-Magnons).[10] The latter has been all alone on this planet ever since. A rough timeline of the likely evolutional history of our kind is shown in Figure 1-1.

The Upright Animal with a Big Brain

Over the long span of history, hominids have thus become increasingly bipedal and terrestrial. The peculiar animal is to balance itself on its two hind legs and hold its large head by a vertical spine. In addition to the anatomical readjustments to its lower limbs, the pelvis itself had to be enlarged and thickened for the weight bearing, and further enlarged in the female for reproduction. Of course, the physical arrangement of carrying a heavy mass on top of a long, narrow tube, which is "the smallest spinal cord relative to his brain... among all the mammals,"[11] has introduced some new vulnerability to the organism. Many physiological difficulties

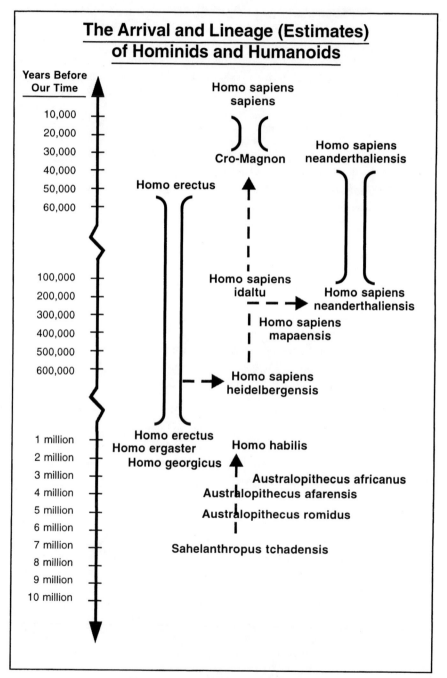

Figure 1-1. The Long Trek

with the head, neck, shoulders, back, knees, and ankles are prevalent in association with bodily misalignments and sudden shifts in movement direction or speed.

Be that as it may, the arboreal-terrestrial conversion decisively freed the forelegs from the weight-carrying and locomotive functions, and the hands with fully opposable thumbs became a unspecialized, multipurpose organ. For example, they can push, pull, poke, punch, chop, slap, grasp, grip, hold, shape, twist, throw, and do many other gross physical operations, but they can also touch, pinch, smooth, rub, and engage in many finer motor movements. Granted that similar observations may be made for many anthropoids, what is unique here is that these most versatile hands have served as the prototypical tool, so to speak, for making all sorts of tools and using them as *extensions* of the very organ that built them. Such extensions may work through the direct motion of the body (e.g., in using the hammer, spade, screw driver, or lever), through a more subtle guiding manipulation (of, e.g., the wheels, a balance, and a telescope), or simply by being in place for utilization (e.g., roads, canals, dams).[12] Regardless of the type of application, the scope of such creations and the pervasiveness of their use clearly distinguish *Homo* from all others.

There is little doubt that the special capability of our hands has played a critical role in shaping the inimitable history of *Homo sapiens*. Nevertheless, how the remarkable versatility of this organ has actually interrelated with the noticeable development of human brains still remains largely hypothetical. While some authors give clear primacy to the hands,[13] others argue that "man's brain was from the beginning far more important than his hands, and its size could not be derived solely from his shaping or using of tools."[14] Kingdon is of the opinion that "the invention of a tool has less implication for brain size than the ability to impart knowledge of its effective use,"[15] especially across generations, and believes "mental quickness, adaptability and aptitude in the teaching and learning of new skills"[16] were the best survival value and, hence, contributory to the further enhancement of the brain. Additionally, mental acuity in social perception and cooperative behavior has been noted by some for its possible evolutionary advantage.[17] The likelihood is that,

> Man was perhaps an image maker and a language maker, a dreamer and an artist, even before he was a toolmaker. At all events, through most of history, it was the symbol, not the tool, that pointed to his superior function. Doubtless the two gifts necessarily developed side by side.[18]

The brain. In any case, it is a fact that, even in contrast with some anthropoids, the members of our species come into the world with a bigger head attached to a relatively small body. "In the newborn human, fully one-seventh of the total weight is brain!,"[19] the body weight being approximately 7 pounds and the brain slightly less than one.

The brain-to-body ratios among such great apes as orang-utans, chimpanzees, and gorillas are roughly 1 to 11-14 (the brain, ca. 0.3 pound; the body, 3.3-4.2). Comparatively, therefore, our newborns come with a brain three times as heavy as that of the great apes, attached to a body only about twice as heavy. Moreover, that big brain grows even heavier relatively soon after birth. Thus, the baby human brain doubles in weight in half a year, and trebles in 2.5 years. It reaches 90 percent of the adult brain weight in 5 years. Once grown up, the brain-to-body proportion becomes about 1 to 40-50 (the brain weight, ca.3.2 pounds), but that ratio is 1 to 135 in the orang-utan, 1 to 185 in the chimpanzee, and 1 to (up to) 450-500 in the gorilla, the brains in all of them being about one pound. Therefore, our brain quadruples in weight by adulthood, but those of the great apes merely triple.

These figures may obscure an important fact that, unlike in other primates, "fully three-quarters of the human brain develops outside the womb" and "only at puberty is the physical maturation of the human brain complete."[20] This arrangement seems forced upon us due to the rapid growth of the brain of the fetus in vivo, which makes the whole birthing process an affair rather fraught with danger. "The largest possible brain ... still has to be born through a pelvis."[21] Even for the enlarged maternal pelvis, and even with such further physiological facilitations as the uterine contraction and cervical dilatation, the fit between the birth canal and the oversized fetal head is very tight. For that reason, if the birth were delayed a certain amount of time beyond the due date, chemical and/or surgical interventions would be indicated to save both the mother and the baby.

In fact, even at full term, every human birth is premature in the relative sense, since all newborns require a year or two of extra-uterine gestation before starting to get over their pronounced helplessness and immaturity. The brain's neural building must continue postpartum, and the provision of proper early experiences by the family is essential for that. The comparative developmental delay makes "the principle in biology called *neoteny*, or 'remaining young'.... peculiarly significant in the case of *Homo sapiens*,"[22] both physiologically and behaviorally. "'Infantilization'—the extravagantly prolonged period of human dependency— is ... at the root of our peculiarly human nature. It means that matured animal instincts are replaced in man by learning and socialization."[23] Such juvenile qualities as playfulness and imagination, if kept alive through life, make a grown person neotenous. As Ashley Montagu noted, whereas "the youth of the chronologically young is a gift; growing young into what others call 'old age' is an achievement, a work of art. It takes time to grow young.... Growing young is a habit best acquired in childhood."[24]

The body. Of course, the anatomical innovations associated with the bipedality and larger brains were not exclusive to hominids, and both had been a long time in the making. A long snout was removed from the creatures who came in from the sea,[25] and the anthropoid muzzles have been shortened in the further reshaping of the heads. And those heads had to be held high on the spine, rather than hung from it. The hominid skulls were made increasingly lighter, the craniums rounder, the teeth smaller, and the jaws drawn in to give the largest possible cubic volume to the brains. Related to the more compact jaws with a set of smaller teeth was a shift from a largely herbivorous diet to a more carnivorous one with higher density nutrients. Also in this anatomical remodeling, the eye sockets were repositioned from the sides to the front to allow a stereoscopic view. Given the vertical posture now habitually adopted by *Homo*, the olfactory sense (i.e., smell) was superseded by the vision as the primary sense with which to take a bearing of the world and of itself.

As observed in the chapter-opening statement of Eiseley, what makes the whole experience unrepeatable is the remarkable conjunction of multiple factors in this history.

> Emancipated hands are not enough: many dinosaurs had them, but they lacked sufficient brains. Intelligence is not enough: elephants have a great deal of intelligence ... but they do not have stereoscopic sights.... Stereoscopic eyes are not enough either: for the intelligent, tree-living apes have them.... It is the combination that counts. Man has paired grasping organs, fully in his field of vision and wholly freed from locomotor duties, in a stereoscopic-sighted, big-brained mammal—and these add up to the answer.[26]

Indeed, it is the combination that counts. A case in point is seen in early hunts for larger prey. In coordination with the hand, which was increasingly adept at making complex tools and wielding powerful weapons, the head had to organize and execute. "Consider what hunting requires: speed and accuracy, obviously, but even more important, the ability to plan, communicate, and cooperate."[27] Moreover, ancestral humans left extraordinary paintings of the animals and hunters in caves like Chauvet, Lascaux, and Altamira, which Bronowski believes to be more for preparation than for reminiscence. The vivid pictures reveal "the ability to visualize the future, to foresee what may happen and plan to anticipate it, and to represent it to [oneself] in images that [one] project[s] and move about inside [one's] head...," in other words, the unique capacity of "forward-looking imagination."[28] It is not irrelevant in this connection that, "Our vision faces what is *ahead* and *in front....* We are so largely oriented toward what is ahead."[29]

Evolution through Culture

In fact, the singularity of human vision has many ramifications. Given that "all through evolution, species have moved from proximity-senses [i.e., touch, taste, and smell] to distance-senses [hearing and sight]..., a rough idea of the evolutionary position of any animal can be gained from knowing merely the repertory and relative development of the animal's senses."[30] Furthermore, the nervous system of modern humans, who live at the confluence of "two quite different kinds of environment, the one more 'natural' and the other more cultural,...evolved under the selective pressures of a hominid line increasingly given over to *cultural adaptations.*"[31]

The ultimate significance of all the anatomical innovations in *Homo* may be found in this, "one momentous fact. An African primate had crossed an entirely new threshold where biological adaptation was overtaken by cultural adaptation."[32] To repeat, yet again,

> Man differs from the rest of the animal kingdom not by his biological endowments but by the use he has made of them, usually in a conscious manner.... He can thus produce works of art, scientific concepts, moral codes, legal systems, and other organizations of experience which constitute the building stones of his psychosocial evolution—a process which is for mankind much more important than biological evolution. To a large extent, mankind is defined by its collective achievements—in other words, by its cultures.[33]

All cultural creations, all the tools and other extensions, have thus come to play a crucial part in human development. "Nothing like this has ever happened before in evolution. Machines not only can do man's flying, diving, and superhuman seeing and hearing for him, but also *they do his evolving for him.*"[34] It is not that anatomy ceased "to be a meaningful manifestation of change, but [that] it became both subordinate to and, to a significant degree, the *consequence* of culture."[35] In that sense, therefore, "culture has become a more efficient and powerful genetic device."[36]

The risk of evolution. Basically, the advantage of the evolution by culture over the evolution by biology is twofold: the former is much (a) safer and (b) faster, than the latter. As is well known, organic evolution proceeds through mutation and natural selection. "All previous animals had been subject to the *autoplastic* evolution of their self-substance, committing their bodies to the experimental adaptations in a blind genetic gamble for survival. The stakes in this game were high: life or death."[37] That is to say, changes occur through mutations. Because of the variations among individuals, some manage to persist and reproduce, while others die out. Thus, only the genes of the survivors are passed on, and the surviving species as a whole will be different than before. "All sorts of mutations occur and it is only those that, *by chance*, enable the organism to survive better that will spread through the species"—accordingly, "the mutations are 'random.'"[38] The results of change are not predictable, and the evolution may not necessarily be adaptive. The once-and-for-all selection cannot be repeated, and it is certainly not reversible.

In contrast, the evolution by culture proceeds by means of experimentation with extensions, i.e., with what humans themselves have created. Therefore, "man's evolution ... is through *alloplastic* experiments with objects outside of his own body and is concerned only with the products of his hands, brains, and eyes—and not with his body itself."[39] Unlike autoplastic experiments, alloplastic ones are both replicable and reversible. For instance, we can navigate a plane in the dark by utilizing a radar without modifying (even if we could) the rod cells in our eyes, and we can address a multitude in a large auditorium or stadium by using a voice amplification system without remodeling our own vocal cord and pulmonary system. If the particular devices do not work, we replace them with different ones, not risking ourselves at all. Similarly, if searching for a sunken ship, we can send a specially built submersible down without endangering any life or somehow altering ourselves into supernatural divers.

The pace of evolution. For obvious reasons, then, the pace of change is much more rapid in the cultural evolution than in the genetic one.

> We human beings do not manufacture new forms via mutation.... The length of time for such a favorable mutation to occur— since the vast majority of mutations are negative...—would be extremely long.... And when it does, that change will be transmitted solely to the specific offspring—and only after hundreds of generations may it enter into the species at large. Cultural changes, on the other hand, can be directly and universally transmitted to everyone in that culture.[40]

The expression that "cultural evolution is Lamarckian and very fast, whereas biological evolution is Darwinian and very slow,"[41] seems to capture the contrast between the two modes of evolution. Indeed, "human beings do transmit acquired characteristics to successive generations—but through our culture rather than our genes."[42]

A good example of the rapidity and safety of evolution by extension is the unbelievably swift development of the whole aero-spatial means of movement. After many millennia of mere fantasy on the part of the organism that was obviously not meant to be air-born, the featherless biped has managed to accomplish the feat of flying in an amazingly short span of time. Barely 500 years after the imaginative designs of Leonardo da Vinci, 220 years from the air balloons of the Montgolfier brothers, and 100 years after the brief flight of the Wright brothers, *Homo sapiens* has successfully launched itself into the vast darkness of the galaxy. From pioneering ventures with life-size kites and wings, handled by human muscles, to more recent experiences with much heavier metal crafts powered by fossil, chemical, nuclear, or solar fuels, the principle of alloplastic experimentation has guided the dramatic change from just another earth-bound animal into a daring, space-exploring creature. This transformation is all the more remarkable in a species that, in terms of biological adaptation, "seems not to be evolving at all since he first appeared as man, except in minor perfectings of his vertical posture."[43]

The comparative features of the two modes of evolution are presented in Table 1-1, and the contrastive significance is nicely summarized in another statement by Weston LaBarre.

> With man, genetic evolution and organic experiments have come to an end. Without involving the animal body and its slow, blind genetic mechanisms, man's hands make the tools and the machines which render his own further physical

evolution unnecessary; they replace the slow, cumbrous, expensive, uncertain, and painful mechanism of organic evolution with the swift, conscious, biologically free, and painless making of machines.[44]

Table 1-1. Two Modes of Human Evolution

HUMAN EVOLUTION	
Through	**Through**
Biology	Culture
Genetics	Extension
Mutation & Natural Selection	Experimentation
Autoplastic	Alloplastic
Slow	Fast
Irreplicable	Replicable
Less Predictable	More Predictable
Irreversible	Reversible

With that in mind, let us take a closer look at the helpful tools and machines and other cultural extensions.

Notes

1. Eiseley, 1957, 160-161.
2. See, e.g., Allman, 1994; Bronowski, 1981; Burke and Ornstein, 1995; Kingdon, 1993; La Barre, 1954.
3. Burke and Ornstein, 1995, 8-9.
4. T. White et al., 1994.
5. Brunet et al., 2002; 2005. Zollikofer et al., 2005. However, subsequent controversies have kept the ancestral status of the discovered fossils unsettled. The key question has to do with whether the creature was truly an obligate biped (hence, hominid) or a quadrupedal ape. See, e.g., Wolpoff et al., 2002; Beauvilan and Le Guellec, 2004.
6. Gore, 2002.
7. Kingdon, 1993.
8. T. White et al., 2003.
9. The interesting story of how ice age served as a springboard for Hominid development is told in such works as Chorlton et al., 1983; Hoyle, 1981; Imbrie and Imbrie, 1979, and Sutcliffe, 1985. The history of glacial cycles and climatic variations continues to be unraveled through on-going research projects—see, e.g., EPICA Group, 2004.
10. Maureille, 2002. The information about who coexisted with whom, when and where, still remains indefinite. See, e.g., P. Brown et al., 2004, on the very recent discovery of the small-bodied *Homo floresiensis* in Indonesia. It is estimated that this direct descendant of *Homo erectus* was co-inhabiting the earth a mere 18,000 years ago, albeit in relative isolation.
11. La Barre, 1954, 77.
12. Rothenberg, 1993.
13. E.g., F. Wilson, 1998.
14. Mumford, 1967, 14.
15. Kingdon, 1993, 36.
16. Ibid., 37.
17. E.g., Allman, 1994.
18. Mumford, 1952, 35.
19. La Barre, 1954, 76.
20. Shore, 1996, 3.
21. La Barre, 1954, 79.
22. Ibid., 303-304.
23. Ibid., 304-305.
24. Montagu, 1983, 194.
25. Eiseley, 1957.
26. La Barre, 1954, 86-87.
27. Burke and Ornstein, 1995, 11.
28. Bronowski, 1981, 33.
29. Erikson, 1974, 88-89.

30. La Barre, 1954, 37.
31. Shore, 1996, 4, 380.
32. Kingdon, 1993, 36.
33. Dubos, 1968, 249-250.
34. La Barre, 1954, 90.
35. Kingdon, 1993, 36.
36. Gaylin, 1991, 37.
37. La Barre, 1954, 90.
38. Lewontin, 2000, 72.
39. La Barre, 1954, 90.
40. Gaylin, 1991, 184.
41. E. Wilson, 1978, 78.
42. Gaylin, 1991, 184.
43. La Barre, 1954, 133.
44. Ibid., 89-90.

Chapter 2. Creations of the Creature

Cultural extensions, we said in Chapter 1, have been a truly distinguishing feature, an inimitable mark, of humankind. Indeed, their creation and uses have become so prevalent as to make us readily forget that life, as most of us know it, is practically unsustainable without them. We take them totally for granted and unsuspectingly believe that they have always been here with us from the beginning of the universe.

For instance, many of our children cannot even imagine a world without televisions, airplanes, computers, and supermarkets, in the same way that we ourselves have had trouble visualizing the "archaic," or even "barbaric," existence of our parents and grandparents lacking telephones, refrigerators, automobiles, or Band-Aids! We often find ourselves at a loss in another culture where merchants will not accept credit cards for payment, or where self-service laundromats are non-existent. Some of us even complain bitterly about those ignorant natives who cannot speak *the* God-given language that is, needless to say, always our own!

David Rothenberg tells a story that addresses this peculiar tendency in all of us: "The machine is always there.... When it takes us to the top of the mountain, we are no longer sure whether we could have walked there ourselves."[1] It would be instructive at this point to look at the many kinds of extensions we have developed in all sectors of life in order to appreciate (1) some salient characteristics of all extensions, and (2) the scope and magnitude of their "enhancement of power" over us, human beings, and our environment.

External or Material Extensions

As noted in Chapter 1, the very prototype of all extensions is the human hand once it was freed from the basic function of body support and locomotion. Among humans, it has become a truly versatile organ, a sort of multi-purpose *tool* or *instrument*, for everyday activities. Our hands with fully opposable thumbs can grasp a big club, hold chopsticks, pick up a thin film, push along a heavy box, stroke a pet, knead clay, slap a face, strike keyboards, hold up a baby, strum chords on a musical instrument, punch/thrust/chop an opponent, scoop up food, clasp a key, pinch a person, scratch nose, and perform innumerable other feats.

Not surprisingly, this idea of tool has remained the easiest way to think of what extensions in general are about. As Jacob Bronowski observed, "From the very beginning of specifically human evolution we have made tools or artifacts to serve our purposes.... The characteristic feature of all human cultures is that they make artifacts; and this is really what we mean when we say that the human mind is creative."[2]

Thus, one major group of extensions comprises all sorts of objects we have made and/or used for instrumental purposes—a category I am calling *external* or *material* extensions.[3] As roughly categorized in Table 2-1, this group includes many varieties of which some are examined below.

Table 2-1. Examples of External or Material Extensions

TOOLS and IMPLEMENTS
GADGETS and INSTRUMENTS
MACHINES and EQUIPMENT
ARMS and WEAPONS
FOODSTUFF
SHELTER and CLOTHING
MEANS of COMMERCE
SOURCES of ENERGY
OBJECTS OF ART

Tools and implements. We are all familiar with sundry household tools such as hammers, screwdrivers, saws, and scissors. As various rooms or spaces of a house typically serve different purposes, one tends to find differing assortments of tools in different areas. In the kitchen, for example, utensils such as pots, pans, bowls, dishes, cups, glasses, knives, and silvers would be quite prominent while, in the yard, gardening implements like shovels, hoes, rakes, clippers, and hoses are amassed. In the work room, we see piles of nails, screws, files, glues, tapes, rules, levels, and vises, in addition to drills, saws, hammers, screw drivers, and the like.

When we think about it, the proliferation of these seemingly simple items is really astounding. I am one of those who has always been finding it impossible to memorize all the different names to identify correctly what I [supposedly] need or want. Therefore, I much appreciated a cartoon, displayed in a neighborhood store, depicting an imaginary hardware store that has only five, clearly marked departments to make customers' lives easy. They are named, respectively, "Doodads," "Thingamajigs," "What's-ya-ma-call-it's," "Dohickeys," and, last but not least, "Whatnots"!

Gadgets and instruments. If you have not been following the more recent developments in the age-old human quest for a better mousetrap, it may be worth your while to pay a visit to such a state-of-the-art(!) hardware store as the one in the above cartoon. You will be amazed by the wide selections ranging from the classic models with a bait hook and a spring to the newer, more "humane" varieties that simply trap your nemesis without killing it outright. The one that particularly impressed me was a gadget called the glue trap—a tiny square pool of transparent, adhesive glue with a couple of enticing morsels floating in the middle. Woe to any mouse lured by the yummy bait to step into the pool, thus getting stuck there forever. The model worked nicely for me, but there was one flaw—what was I supposed to do with the animal so trapped?

The point of all this is that one of the notable features of cultural extensions is their *specificity*. That is to say, each extension typically specializes in a singular function, and performs a very specific operation and little else. Unlike the human hand, which has developed into a multi-purpose organ, most things created by that multi-functional hand provide us with only a *selectively accentuated* power for a particular purpose. For instance, saws are not a choice tool for hammering, and deep pots are a poor substitute for frying pans. One is helpless with a larger screwdriver in trying to fix a small instrument like a wrist watch. This fact has many ramifications in life, and shall be a topic of discussion in Chapter 3.

Back to gadgets and instruments, it is again easy to spot many of these in any home environment. Two inventions, related to each other, are indeed classic—the calendar and the clock. Humans have been spending much time and efforts in developing and refining these but, in that very process, each has come to perform only its own specialized function, more or less independently of the other. Even for that reason alone, many of the magnificent Renaissance creations that combine an understanding of the workings of the heavens with a mastery of necessary mechanics continue to astound us. One example is the masterpiece mounted in 1410 on the east wall of the old town hall of Prague, Czech Republic, which shows not only the time of the day but also the phase of the moon and the positions of the planets. Every hour on the hour, moreover, a figure of death appears in the window brandishing its scythe and shaking its hour-glass. The twelve disciples file by, followed by Christ himself, and finally by a Turk, who shakes his head as if he were still pursuing his dream of the eternal Ottoman empire!

Of course, there was also the remarkable invention of wheels and, later, that of ball bearings, which have changed, among others, the transportation scene forever. Note that the *specificity* feature was operating here again. Thus, it is a peculiar fact of history that the Mayan people, for all their highly developed mathematical-astronomical knowledge *with* many complex, circular representations and calendrical derivations, apparently never grasped "the underlying principle of the wheel"[4] to see the possibility of using those same wheels in pulleys and carts to build their magnificent cities.

One other item in this category of gadgets and instruments merits a special mention, because it exemplifies some other characteristics of extensions. The invention in question is that of the optical lens. Thanks to that tiny piece of glass (and, later, plastic), many of us nowadays wear eyeglasses or contact lenses to "correct" our faulty vision, enabling us to go about our business without too much difficulty. Before this invention, however, any failing eyesight doomed a person at no matter what age—an experience to be truly dreaded. So, enhancing one's organismic power through extensions also means a certain degree of *equalization* among people of differing capabilities. With velcros and zippers, even very young children can now handle their coats and shoes where they used to have much trouble handling buttons and shoelaces.

Meanwhile, unfortunately, some wimps may feel all powerful and superior with, say, a switchblade knife or a handgun to do much harm to other people. More gratifying examples can be seen in quite a few disabled persons enjoying active sports like the basketball and skiing with the help of prosthetic gear. Also, some of the multiple-handicapped can nowadays see, talk, and write with a special headwear and a computer-assisted typewriter, or other similar devices.[5]

Now, what may be called the *procreation* effect of extension is readily seen in the subsequent elaboration of the original lens, that is, in the refinement and further development of the *primary* (i.e., initial) extension. When, allegedly, Galileo Galilei put together two lenses slightly apart to make a telescope, people were introduced to a *secondary* (derivative) extension that augmented the visual power even further. The same goes for another secondary extension, microscope, developed by Zacharias Jansen. The *tertiary* extensions in the respective realms of exploration have included radio telescopes and electron microscopes. Thus, one extension tends to give rise to many progenies, generation after generation. [Note, however, that it is a poor idea to go get a microscope to look at stars, or a telescope to study microorganisms, due to the *specificity* effect.]

Machines and equipment. Of course, all the above-mentioned effects apply to yet another, major category of extensions that subsumes all sorts of machines for production (e.g., looms, gins, mills, and printing machines), for communication (typewriters, telegrams, telephones, televisions, etc.), for transportation (e.g., aqueducts, water wheels, belt conveyors, elevators, bridges, ferries, trains, automobiles, ships, balloons, and airplanes), and for other functions.

In looking at picture books with our mechanically-inclined son, for instance, we were surprised to discover the existence of previously unsuspected varieties of heavy road equipment. Both the child and the parents learned, for the first time, what the backhoe excavator, goose neck crane, face shovel, or roadheader looks like, what each does do, and how every one of them is different from all others. Likewise, in the realm of trains, we came across the flat cars and gondola cars and box cars and hopper cars and many many others, all developed for specialized purposes, often as a result of the procreation dynamics of extension.

Arms and weapons. Necessity is, it has been said, the mother of invention. Whether we like it or not, *Homo* has been engaging itself long and hard in hunts, combats, battles, and warfare. In that process, we have invented an astounding number of arms and weapons, varying in purpose, size, complexity, and power. Starting probably with a simple stick, rock, or string, these extensions have come to include bows and arrows, knives and swords, spears and axes, traps and poisons, guns and canons, bombs and mines, tanks and rockets, and warships and warplanes. A high-ranking general in charge of Russia's strategic rocket forces was quoted to observe the irony of the whole process: "You cannot stop the human mind. Unfortunately, men will always be driven to create new weapons. We expend our ingenuity inventing new systems and then have to work to find ways to eliminate them."[6]

Also ironically, the never-ending search for "better" weapons, meaning more efficient, powerful, and effective means of capture, destruction, injury, and death, has historically given birth to many a by-product and/or derivative extension that is beneficial in the civilian life. A classic example may be the better quality steel initially sought after for weaponry, but also quite useful for everyday cutlery or ubiquitous ball bearings. Jet engines now powering most long distance commercial flights had their immediate ancestors in the dreadful engines of mass destruction in the Second World War, known as the German V-1 and V-2 rockets, as well as rocket- or jet-powered fighter planes like Messerschmidt 163 (Komet) and 262. Similarly, the safety of aerial and nautical navigation today owes much to the military efforts on radar and sonar development during the same world conflict.

Numerous other byproducts of war have likewise enriched our daily life in forms such as fabrics (e.g., the rip-stop nylon for clothing, suitcases, tents, etc.); gadgets (a small water purifying pump, a specialized watch for sea- or sky-divers, and the like); optical equipment (night vision binoculars, miniature cameras, etc.); and food processing (freeze drying and so on). In some cases, even the products of failed research have turned out quite useful for unintended purposes. The "killer ray," which could not zap the original targets like planes, ships, tanks, or soldiers, has given rise to the convenient microwave oven and, though not military in origin, the glue that did *not* stick gave us the handy "Post'em" memo sheets.

Foodstuff. As regards what we consume, it is remarkable to see that practically nothing is really "natural" any longer. Even where "health" or "organic" food is promoted for its alleged naturalness, the fact of human intervention in nature is everywhere unmistakable. While "successful farming, like gardening, is incompatible with the ecological equilibrium that would exist under natural conditions," as noted by Rene Dubos, "the human presence can enrich the creativeness of nature [by replacing] the spontaneous blind processes of nature [with] the changes guided or imposed by human choices and decisions."[7]

The shift from the hunter-gatherer mode of food access to the farming mode was a giant step for the humankind. Selected plants were consciously and routinely cultivated and, in time, certain genetic principles (e.g., those identified by Gregor Mendel in the mid-19th century) came to be intentionally tapped for new, more desirable breeds. The work of Luther Burbank epitomized the magic of hybridization and, more recently, the efforts of Norman Borlaug (the 1970 Nobel Peace Laureate) showed how selective breeding may help stem the scourge of worldwide starvation by giving birth to a faster growing, blight-resistant variety of wheat with higher yields. So, mighty farm equipment and machinery, or improved fertilizers and insecticides, are not the only extensions upon which modern agriculture draws. Considered interventions by humans have similarly enhanced animal husbandry, fishery, horticulture, and forestry.

Of course, the whole processing and preservation of foodstuff, as well as the packaging and marketing of such products, represents yet another enterprise replete with human interventions. Revealingly, it is hard for many of us to realize that frozen food, dried food, pulverized food, canned food, freeze-dried food, and even TV dinners were *not* among the original manna from Heaven! For that reason, this is a good place to talk about another feature of extensions, which I am calling their *snowballing* effects.

Whenever an extension comes into being, it not only induces further elaboration and refinement of that particular line of creation (described as the *procreation* effect) but also triggers a plethora of related inventions, turning the initial efforts into a conglomerate enterprise. This is *snowballing* effect.

Think, for example, of canned food. To make possible such a derivative extension, one must first presume an underlying development in mining and metallurgy. As an important extension, the creation of alloys has indeed had a long history, having been "discovered after the time of the birth of Christ in South America, and long before that in Asia."[8] Beyond that, however, the technology of milling, cutting, and soldering must have been ready for the production and sealing of metal containers. Similarly, the practice of cleaning and sterilizing, both of the foodstuff and of the container, needed to be well established (as in the precursory folk "canning" with jars, pots, wax, etc.).

Suppose we have managed to produce cans or tins and to have some meat, fruit, or vegetable successfully canned. Since people cannot tell the contents of one sealed can from those of another, some means of identification must obviously be found to mark the container, perhaps by embossing, stamping, or painting on the cans themselves, or by printing labels on paper or fabric and somehow affixing them onto the can (which calls for a suitable glue). In quantities, these cans must now be packed and again labeled in some way, and adequate modes of storage and shipping have also to be devised. Moreover, to change the consumer habits of food consumption, the requirements for publicity and instruction need to be addressed. The list goes on almost ad infinitum. Thus, each extension is closely meshed with other extensions, giving rise to an impressive array of new inventions and contrivances.

Another case in point may be found in the more recent computer business. Once the machine itself (the "hardware") had been built, there arose an immediate need for proper programs (the "software") and accompanying instruction manuals. In addition, all sorts of "peripherals" have had to be developed to sustain and expand the industry. Some of these items are operational necessities (e.g., floppy discs, rechargeable batteries, connecting cables, printing ribbons, inks, and papers); others are conveniences (AC adaptors, battery chargers, "mouse," surge suppressors, monitor screen filters, note holders, disc labels/sleeves/files, orthopedic chairs, keyboard wrist cushions, computer/printer stands, security locks, dust covers, carrying cases, etc.); still others are largely vanity items (e.g., "your own" exclusive name plates, personalized manual covers, desk top organizers with a mug holder, and the like). Obviously, the speed and scope of the snowballing have been remarkable here.

Shelter and clothing. From the initial utilization of naturally formed caves and covers, humans have long ventured into the construction of sheltering walls, roofs, doors, and windows, each architectural feature being a noteworthy extension. Further derivative creations have given birth to both moveable and stationary shelters of all sizes and shapes, as well as to varieties of furniture pieces that go inside them. Tents, tepees, and caravans are still widely used and being refined in many parts of the world. From early wickiups and sod shanties to modern collective tenements and individual houses, and from age-old temples, shrines, mosques, and cathedrals to contemporary sky-scrapers, all sorts of materials and designs have been utilized to build shelters for goods, animals, humans, and even gods. This has given rise to "the genius of the city,"[9] which is the concentration of people and resources. So, the strength of the city was "in its assemblage of the greatest possible variety of skills, aptitudes, interests. Instead of ironing out human differences and standardizing human responses ... the city recognized and emphasized differences."[10]

Or, think of the giant steps that marked transitions from open cess pits to outhouses to chamber pots to indoor privies to water closets, and finally to indoor plumbing. Even with all these procreation efforts, and even for the bourgeoisie, the last step was not to be climbed "until the middle of the nineteenth century [because] most people had no access to centrally supplied [pressurized] water."[11] In other words, that final transition had to wait until the snowballing effects managed to place all the necessary extensions in place.

Similarly, from Adam's and Eve's fig leaves and later loin-cloths to the present-day clothing, humans have been ceaselessly working to develop materials for functional protection against the elements and also, of course, for expressive social display. The varieties of dress items and paraphernalia found in modern stores are quite impressive. As the seasons and vogues change, specialized inventories are introduced to create and satisfy people's needs and wants.

When, for example, a friend of mine who is an enthusiastic runner took me to a store filled with "athletic" shoes, I was dumbfounded to see all the special purpose shoes for simple walking, jogging, sprinting, long-distance running, hiking, mountaineering, rock climbing, sailing, tennis, basketball, racketball, and ad infinitum. Since I do not engage myself in any such sports and, as a matter of fact, own only one pair of seldom worn, outdated sneakers, the experience was a revelation. Obviously, for both functional and display purposes, any serious sportsperson *must* have a full line of proper footwear. A man or woman may be for all seasons, but a pair of shoes is just for a particular time and a given exercise!

Means of commerce. In dealing with this sort of "embarrassment of riches," we have also developed quite varied and intricate modes of transaction. The initial and long-standing practice of bartering gradually gave way to the use of intermediary devices of tokens and money. Metallic coins seem to have originated in China, India, and Asia Minor in the 7th and 6th centuries, B.C. Likewise, the introduction of money orders and cheques, and later of credit cards, has drastically changed the commercial mode of transaction. Most recently, of course, the electronic contrivances of fund transfer are making it possible for some people to move about and do business even without paper money, chequebooks, or plastic cards. Still, world travellers are often reminded of the newness of these derivative extensions when they find themselves in "cash only" societies.

Sources of energy. Whenever major storms cause power failure, we are shocked to realize how much we have taken electricity for granted, how dependent we have become on the ready and continuous availability of this energy source, and how unprepared we are with the provision of an alternative power supply, even such a simple one as a candle with some matches. Like modern-day children who believe that milk comes from supermarkets (not cows), many adults behave as if electricity originates in wall switches!

As is well known, the discovery of fire was a true turning point in the history of *Homo.* In point of fact, however, the real significance lay in the discovery of the *portability* or *reproducibility* (that is to say, the controllability) of this mysterious natural phenomenon. The beginning uses might have been of wood (and charcoal), to be followed by peat, vegetable oil, animal fat, coal, petroleum, and natural gas.

Coal powered the First Industrial Revolution of mid-18th through early 19th centuries. In the Second Industrial Revolution that began in the late 19th century, however, derivative extensions were the "new" energy sources—first the steam power, then electricity. Needless to say, both inventions enormously augmented the power of the creative creature.

Unlike the age-old utilization of the power of water, the cultivation of the wind, tide, sun, or volcano as a practical source of energy has not so far been as uniformly successful. Meanwhile, the magnetic energy (antigravity or levitation) is just about ready to power experimental high-speed trains. The latest and most potent nuclear energy still remains in its infancy as regards its manageability with all the attendant fear of the unknown.

Objects of art. Last but certainly not least, our species has made a large number of objects that appear less directly instrumental than most of the extensions in the foregoing categories. The seemingly ubiquitous, small human or animal figures are a classic case in point. Made of sticks or straws, these are typically found in archeological sites of early settlements or burial grounds, side by side with more obviously utilitarian items. People continue to puzzle over the functions of such simple and often crude objects, and wonder whether they served recreational purposes as playthings, instructional purposes as models, decorative purposes for the domicile or the person, religious purposes, or anything else.

Whatever the answer might be, there has been a plenitude of fetishes, amulets, icons, masks, paintings, sculptures, books, toys, and other artifacts in human lives. Music and dance are interesting subcategories in that, at the point of original creation, both are far more ephemeral, if not intangible, than most others listed above. For a long time, even the pieces of "instrumental" music had to be preserved by memory in the so-called oral tradition. Granted, the secondary extensions of coding and notating systems and, nowadays, recording technologies (phonograph, film, audio and video cassettes, CD's, DVD's, etc.) have presented the immense possibility for reproduction of the sounds and movements. However, even such technological *re*creation is in many ways not the same as the initial, live, fleeting acts. For most of the human past, musical and dance experiences were indeed a passing parade, leaving no artifacts behind.

In general, it may be argued that the human creations in this category of art objects represent the most obvious link between the *material or external* extensions and the *nonmaterial or internal* ones. Certainly, things like military, sporting, or scouting medals and badges, trophies and monuments, or diplomas, certificates, etc., are the secondary, material extensions of such primary, nonmaterial extensions as honors, distinctions, and titles.

Let us now turn to the examination of the latter variety.

Internal or Nonmaterial Extensions

Even a cursory survey of material inventions makes us realize the immense scope of what we ourselves have created and utilized everywhere for hundreds of thousands of years all over the earth. Truly, human beings live and die by such extensions, which interlock with and augment each other, proliferating unbelievably swiftly. As observed in Chapter 1, this strange creature known as *Homo sapiens* has enhanced its relatively limited powers as an organism to become a predominant animal on earth. That is mostly how the species has been changing and evolving itself—the way of cultural evolution, or of evolution via prosthesis.

Although the pervasiveness of these tangible handiworks and the immensity of their influence are quite phenomenal, extensions of a nonmaterial or internal nature (see Table 2-2) prove to be even more dazzling in its scope and effects, especially in relation to the enhancement of power over people, including both ourselves and others. The reason for this lies in the uniqueness of the brainwork of *Homo sapiens*.

Table 2-2. Examples of Internal or Nonmaterial Extensions

CODES
MENTAL CONSTRUCTIONS
SOCIAL CONVENTIONS
SOCIAL STRUCTURES

Between the receptor system and the effector system, which are to be found in
all animal species, we find in man a third link which we may describe as the
symbolic system.... No longer in a merely physical universe, man lives in a
symbolic universe. Language, myth, art, and religion are parts of this universe.
They are the varied threads which weave the symbolic net, the tangled web of
human experience.... This new acquisition transforms the whole of human life.
As compared with the other animals man lives not merely in a broader reality;
he lives, so to speak, in a new *dimension* of reality.[12]

Codes. The most obvious category of internal extensions subsumes all sorts
of codes developed and used by humans. The prototype of such creations is the
codified vocalizations that take the place of individual grunts, groans, cries, yells,
and other utterances and exclamations. As a primary extension, certain words are
agreed upon in a given group to designate particular things, places, or events, and
to summarize one's sensations, emotions, acts, or experiences. That is why *all*
children in the English-speaking world learn to sneeze, "Ah-choo!," and yell,
"Ouch!" to any physical hurt.

Any code is obviously of human creation, and it is learned and used by the
interested parties for social reasons. Oral language depends upon such words and
agreed-upon rules, tacit or explicit, for their usage. Still, one occasionally hears of
a "private" code developed by some twins or siblings in their early years to give
them a means of communication that is often indecipherable to anybody else.
"Secret" codes are routinely and intentionally created and maintained by the
military, business-industrial, or diplomatic corps. And, indeed, to those who have
not learned the particular language, any *foreign* tongue remains essentially a secret
and an enigma.

At the primary extension level, people already derive benefit from their
collective resources and experiences. For instance, instead of remaining isolated
and being totally dependent upon one's own devices, an individual can now receive
cues and warnings of an imminent danger from the *community* of people. "Watch
out!" "Fire!" "Hit the deck!" "Stop!" "Jump!" "Help!" and other similar, simple
pronouncements can already inform and direct a person much more clearly and
efficiently than inarticulate grunts or cries. This function of extensions is essentially
a matter of utilizing other people's nervous systems in addition to one's own.[13]

Of course, oral instructions of more elaborate nature can further the beneficial
effects and make it easier, for example, to follow the right trail, build a cabin
properly, or bake a cake right. Alfred Korzybski "defined man *functionally* as a
time-binder" because, in such a manner, "each generation of humans, at least
potentially, can start where the former generation left off."[14] Time-binders are
"capable of 'binding' into their own experience the abstracts of other persons,
other nervous systems, not only those now living but also those who lived in times
long past."[15]

By the time the secondary extension of written code has been developed, the invention crosses over into the material/external category. The code is now visible, and it is far less transitory than the oral version. Things recorded in written codes can be preserved and utilized much more easily across time than orally transmitted stories, which tend to be lost, changed, or forgotten. Therefore, the written versions may continue to entertain and inform people across many a historical epoch. In fact, the transition from the oral communication of knowledge to the written recording is the usual demarcation point between prehistory and history of humankind.

"All living organisms die: through the mind alone man in some degree survives and continues to function.... The mind reproduces itself by transmitting its symbols to other intermediaries, human and mechanical, than the particular brain that first assembled them."[16] The advantage of time-binding is quite obvious in the record of events, and the same may of course be said of the power of notations in music, as well as in dance and movement in general. We should also remember the parallel function of *space-binding* in which what originated in one locale, one region, one nation, or one continent changes, and continues to change, people's lives elsewhere and, frequently, everywhere. A map serves as a good case in point, guiding voyagers from all places in an unfamiliar territory, an unknown hemisphere, and so on. Together, time- and space-binding would work essentially like the legendary "time machine," allowing people to transcend the confines of their particular historical and geographical life contexts.

At the secondary level of extension, codes, whether linguistic or otherwise, are further systematized and made quite tangible. However, while powerful as a means for recording and communicating, these formal codes would be of little use or significance to anyone uninitiated. This aspect of the specificity effect of extensions is easy to see when one thinks of missives spelled out in the hieroglyph, Chief Sequoya's Cherokee alphabet, the Braille system, the differing "sign languages" for the deaf, Morse Code, semaphores, the chemical and mathematical symbols, or the musical and dance notations. To be illiterate in any such codes is to be left out.

Interestingly, this very feature has often been used for the purpose of group identification, or for differentiating outsiders (*them*) from insiders (*us*). For example, gang membership is typically indicated through certain "lingo," manners of gesticulation, movement, clothing, or insignia. To anybody not belonging to the particular gang or its rivals, such codes would mean little. To the outsider, likewise, all graffiti are merely a look-alike eye-sore, but they do convey a clear message to those who are in the relevant groups and hence in the know.

As another example, it is unlikely for people to entrust a large ship in the hands of somebody who orders the craft steered "left or right," or directs sailors "upstairs or downstairs." People are in trouble if the captain does not know to what "sheet" refers aboard a sailing vessel, or cannot respond to maritime flag signals. For that reason, an important part of any specialization rests in learning how to "talk right." Every occupation has its own jargon, and a person must at least learn that formalized code before being accorded a full membership. In other words, lawyers must talk "legalese" to be believable, and doctors must use "medicalese" to be plausible.

Finally, one must recognize the special function of the numbers among the various codes developed over the centuries. Counting and accounting of goods, animals, and people by the use of tokens has had a long history,[17] while the shift from the Roman style of number writing to the Arabic notation was a remarkable innovation with the introduction of the decimal system and the number 0 (zero).[18] Beyond its clear role in commerce, the lasting significance of numerical symbols lay in the fact that "only when the habit of using mathematical abstractions became ingrained in a dominant part of the community could the physical sciences"[19] and technology develop to further the pursuit of the perennial human dreams of power, wealth, and immortality.

Mental constructions. Another major category includes all sorts of ideas and other mental constructions—all abstract yet quite powerful in consequence. Carl Sandburg noted, "Nothing happens unless first a dream,"[20] while Dubos put the same idea in prose, saying, "Mankind's greatest achievements are the products of vision."[21] Indeed, visions, dreams, and images, as well as memories, have exerted so much influence on human lives as to be acknowledged as truly remarkable constructions. Such an "improbable idea [as] taming and then riding the horse,"[22] as making garments out of silkworm's cocoons, or as flying through the air ourselves, has unmistakably changed the course of human history.

Of course, many ideas that are not teleological have also helped mold the particular shape of who we are today. Inferential ideas, be they developed deductively, inductively, or intuitively,[23] constitute one large group. Examples might include ancient concepts in mathematics like irrational numbers, negative numbers, and number zero; or more recent concepts in physics like matter waves, relativity, and quarks. In the social realm, such concepts as fate, equality, and race have had considerable impact worldwide.

Then, there is the "traditional logic" that allows us to "comprehend ... those objects which are free from contradiction, and which have a consistent nature and truth." Alas, as to be discussed in Chapter 7, "it is ... just this homogeneity which we never find in man."[25]

In the face of the conundrum of life, *Homo sapiens* has also invented analogy (such as simile and metaphor). With this device, we make sense of the unfamiliar and unknown by relating them to the familiar and known. In fact, "our ordinary conceptual system, in terms of which we both think and act, is fundamentally metaphorical in nature" [26] [For further discussion, see Chapter 6.]

Furthermore, the species has everywhere created myths to explain its existential meaning. "A myth is a statement about society and man's place in it and in the surrounding universe.... [As such,] its 'scientific truth' or otherwise is irrelevant,"[27] while its explanatory power is incontrovertible. We may not be clearly aware of the particular myth we believe in, but myths underlie every world view

(*Weltanschauung*), every ideology, and every civilization.

Another mental construct of extraordinarily pervasive power is the concept or image of self. As a singular "life aware of itself,"[28] humans have scrutinized themselves, formed self-concepts and then, for better or worse, come under the sway of these very notions about themselves.

> There is danger as well as wisdom ... in such self-scrutiny.... [Man] can define and redefine his own humanity, his own conception of himself. In so doing, he may give wings to the spirit or reshape himself into something more genuinely bestial than any beast of prey obeying its own nature. In this ability to take on the shape of his own dreams, man extends beyond visible nature into another and stranger realm.[29]

Finally, let us remember that everyday experiences like anxiety, shame, remorse, and guilt are uniquely of human creation. So far as we know, lions do not stay awake feeling guilty about the victims of the day's hunt and feast, and reindeers do not torment themselves with a sense of regret over "The Road Not Taken" a long time ago. Only the peculiar creature, we ourselves, is open to the complementary effects of internal and external extensions. That is to say, the same purpose may be served by either material extensions or nonmaterial extensions, or more often by a combination of both. For instance, to insure personal safety against certain untoward social behaviors, one can set up fences, walls, doors, and locks, thus changing the environment by these external creations. One can also attain the same goal by altering people internally through the mental construction of conscience. "Walls, doors, and locks [are] a physical extension of morality— externalization of processes handled internally...."[30]

Of course, most of us would like to use both varieties of protection simultaneously for security. Similarly, the sense of national pride and loyalty inside a person may be accentuated on the outside by displaying such material extensions as flags, patriotic songs, medals, T-shirt slogans, yellow ribbons, or other suitable clothing ornaments. Likewise, pendants (e.g., a cross), pins, car ornaments (a fish sign, bumper stickers, etc.), or books of sacred literature often serve to back up one's faith and devotion. More collectively, in both examples, the material extensions of statues, monuments, icons, and some other architectural creations further augment the effects of nonmaterial creations.

Social conventions. Over time, peoples on earth have developed differing customs, manners, mores, and taboos to regulate social interactions, and each has adopted these as *the* correct way to behave. When systematized and made explicit, they may constitute a formal "code of conduct," but they work mostly implicitly within the process of socialization. Thus, speaking of "the immense journey" of *Homo sapiens*, Eiseley had this to say:

> This emergent creature was not whole, was not made truly human until, in infancy,

the dreams of the group, the social constellation amidst which his own orbit was cast, had been implanted in the waiting, receptive substance of his brain.[31]

Obviously, all the social *whats* and *hows* are conventions invented by humans within their particular historical-ecological contexts. Their presence is universal, even though the exact substance of such conventions varies from one people to another. "The most important thing for a person to know is just how appropriate a bit of behavior or communication is, and how to respond to it appropriately"[32] In fact, the appropriateness of acts or expressions, which are expected of a person in a given setting is often quite opaque. The so-called roles, even when overtly stated as in job specifications, seldom convey their covert contents. Occasionally serious gaffs in diplomatic protocols, or embarrassing missteps in everyday interactions, stem from that difficulty, thus betraying the regulatory powers of social conventions.

Meanwhile, all sorts of rites and rituals have also been very important in human communal life. "The original purpose of ritual was to create order and meaning where none existed; to affirm them when they have been achieved; to restore them when they were lost.... [Thus,] ritual pervades life."[33] Large scale displays of the cohesive power of rites and rituals are often seen in mass rallies and group movements, be they in athletics (e.g., the opening and closing ceremonies of the Olympics), religion (evangelical "crusades," etc.), performing arts (e.g., the movement choirs, carnivals, concerts), the military (tattoos, and the like), or political demonstrations.

Social structures. One final cluster of nonmaterial extensions has to do with how we organize ourselves into groups, large and small, for various purposes. Referring to early hunting parties, Bronowski reminded us that, "Hunting requires conscious planning and organization by means of language, as well as special weapons.... The hunt is a communal undertaking of which the climax, but only the climax, is the kill."[35] As is the case with any other joint activities, the critical elements of the enterprise here were "communion, communication, and cooperation," the three cornerstones of tribal or village culture.[36]

In time, however, the intimate communal pattern was replaced by increasingly larger, more hierarchical organizational structures that subsume more people, more territory, and more resources. The power of all sorts—political, economic, military, etc.—came to be centralized, and the mode of operation became more standardized and impersonal. The on-going efforts towards the full European Union is re-enacting much of that process. Some new laws and institutions are formed, while the extant ones are revised, reorganized, realigned, or abolished. Additional layers of regulatory agencies and functionaries are initiated, and a common currency has been introduced. Attempts are being made to coordinate disparate systems of yore in such areas as justice, defense, finance, commerce, transportation, and communication, and so on and so forth. What is important to remember is that all such social structures are of the human creation.

Obviously, regardless of the specific overall structure, the purpose of the social grouping may be task-oriented, for example for defense and security, manufacturing, politics, schooling, curing, and so on. Or, it may be more morale-related: welfare (aiding and caring for people), religion, arts, recreation, etc. Groups may be small or large, homogeneous or heterogeneous, temporary or long-standing. Thus, small, temporary, but well-chosen groups may be quite functional in morale-oriented missions and/or in task performance. Emergency medical or rescue teams, or the Special Forces in Armed Services, may come to mind. On the other hand, they may not have enough human and material resources or stability to sustain and expand what they managed to accomplish. In contrast, larger, more heterogeneous, and more permanent groups may be better prepared for such tasks of organization and maintenance. They, however, are prone to become bureaucratic and static. "[Bureaucracy] originates nothing: its function is to pass on, without alteration or deviation, the orders that come from above, from central headquarters."[37] Accordingly, the *instrumentality* for innovation and change and the *institutionality* for orderliness and continuity remain forever in a paradoxical concatenation.[38]

Recapitulation

Now, after all this inventorying, cursory as it has necessarily been, certain summary statements may be made.

a) *Homo sapiens*, over the course of time, has created many an *extension*, both material and nonmaterial, tangible and intangible, external and internal, to enhance its organismic functions.

b) These creations, inventions, or contrivances *augment* the unique creature's *power*, and *extend* its *control* over itself and its environment. Because of this empowering feature, they also equalize people of differing capacities, at least to a certain extent.

c) In addition to the *equalization* effect mentioned above, the extensions show several characteristic features, including the following:

  (i) the *specificity* or *selective accentuation* effect—each extension typically specializing in a singular function for a very specific purpose, thus accentuating the power in a selective manner;

  (ii) the *procreation* effect—an original (primary) extension being continually refined and elaborated upon, thus yielding numerous derivative (secondary, tertiary, etc.) extensions;

  (iii) the *snowballing* effect—each extension triggering the development of many other extensions in related enterprises; and

  (iv) the *complementarity* effect—an external/material extension complementing the function of an internal/nonmaterial extension, or vice versa, for the same purpose.

d) Accordingly, the extensions tend to multiply themselves, interlock with each other, and spread wide and fast through a culture. As a result, the extensions are pervasive in human life, and their aggregate influence over their creators has been enormous.

Indeed, the collective creativity of *Homo sapiens,* exhibited in all such creations, is truly something to behold. Not surprisingly, therefore, people have been proud and fond of these achievements of theirs, and they are eager to enjoy the fruits of their labor. The sentiments were echoed by, among others, novelist Edith Wharton in a work published in 1919, wherein she spoke of "the instinct of every people to value and preserve what they have themselves created and made beautiful.... That is the very key to the secret of reverence; the tenderness we feel for our own effort extending to respect for all fine human effort."[39]

In one sense, what has been called human culture is none other than the sum total of these extensions and how humans *relate* to such creations of their own, as well as how humans *relate* to each other, themselves, and their environment *via* extensions. As great and undeniable as the benefits of human brainwork and handiwork have been, when we carefully examine the nature and character of the double relationships surrounding extensions, we see some inherent dangers and attendant difficulties. In the next chapter, we shall consider the dark lining in the silver cloud.

Notes

1. Rothenberg, 1993, 27.
2. Bronowski, 1978, 64-65.
3. Rothenberg, 1993, presents a similar scheme of dual categories, which he calls, respectively, "the extension of action" and "the extension of thought."
4. Gaylin, 1991, 35.
5. A striking example may be found in Stephen Hawking, Lucasian Professor of Mathematics at the University of Cambridge, England, a chair earlier held by none other than Isaac Newton. In spite of his severe physical strictures, he has managed to express his original ideas with the help of some powerful material extensions at his disposal.
6. Schofield and Smith, 2000.
7. Dubos, 1982, 158, 162-163.
8. Bronowski, 1981, 15.
9. W. White, 1970, 384.
10. Mumford, 1967, 231.
11. Rybczynski, 1987, 129.
12. Cassirer, 1944, 24-25.
13. Hayakawa, 1964, 11.
14. Korzybski, 1948, 39.
15. W. Johnson, 1946, 164.
16. Mumford, 1967, 28.
17. Burke and Ornstein, 1995, 42ff.
18. Bronowski, 1981, 106-107.
19. Mumford, 1967, 278.
20. Sandburg, 1960, 72.
21. Dubos, 1968, 238.
22. Bronowski, 1981, 15.
23. Polanyi, 1962.
24. E.g., Furet, 1994.
25. Cassirer, 1944, 11.
26. Lakoff and Johnson, 1980, 3.
27. Middleton, 1967, x.
28. Fromm, 1974, 92.
29. Eiseley, 1969, 182.
30. Hall, 1977, 28.
31. Eiseley, 1957, 121.
32. Lomax, 1968, 12.
33. Mumford, 1967, 62.
34. E.g., Toepfer, 1998.

35.   Bronowski, 1981, 28.
36.   Mumford, 1967, 163.
37.   Ibid., 201.
38.   Wheelis, 1959.
39.   Wharton, 1919, 36-37.

Chapter 3. Falls the Shadow

For all their pervasiveness and potency, cultural extensions do reveal some peculiarities that can spell weaknesses. Like the *monster* created by Dr. Frankenstein in Mary Shelley's 1881 story,[1] our powerful creations may come to hold sway over us with their enormous potential for both good and evil. When handled without a proper awareness of their shortcomings, they can readily become our master, rather than our servant, to do much harm. Let us therefore take a closer look at some of the features of extensions that surround us and permeate our daily life.

Focusing

The irony, as already noted in Chapter 2, is that these human creations have not matched the multiple functionality of the brains and hands that created them. Edward Hall labeled this the "extension-omission factor," defining it as "the incapacity of any extension to reproduce all the functions of the organ or activity that is extended."[2] Any extension, in other words, is fundamentally a *selective accentuation* of a single organismic function, or a few at best, for a limited purpose, and this specificity is both its boon and its bane. Extensions may indeed be powerful, yet typically not remarkably flexible or versatile.

The double-edged nature of the focusing effects can be readily seen in all walks of life. For instance, those oft-spoofed domestic cleaners, who do sinks but do *not* do windows, can leave behind an immaculately clean kitchen encased by totally dirty, grimy windows out of which nothing may be seen. Over the years, for instance, we have asked our favorite carpenter to do many odd jobs, fixing things up and remodeling in and around our house. He is a totally trustworthy person and a superb craftsman, but he absolutely refuses to undertake one activity, namely, painting of any size, any sort. This has caused quite a bit of consternation in us, since we ourselves cannot even remotely qualify as do-it-yourselfers.

The focusing effects may also be called the *specialization* effects. To cite an example, it has been noticed that many illnesses appear to go undetected even by skilled health care professionals who would not, or could not, look beyond their respective areas of expertise. Like the drunk who looks around for his lost coin under a street lamp, because the light is good there, rather than where he or she actually dropped it, a specialist may confine his or her attention to the area familiar to him or her, thereby running the risk of overlooking inimical conditions lurking right next to it, sometimes until too late. *Focusing*, in other words, also means *exclusion* of, and *inattention* to, what has not been so selected as the focal point. In the case of medical specialists, such inattention seems to be correlated with the profession's increasing reliance on technology (i.e., extensions) and the concomitant loss of direct "connection ... with the patient" and of "the skills and insights [about the treatment of the whole person] that predominated in the previous stage [of medical practice]."[3]

Cultural extensions typically work like such specialists, who have sometimes been caricatured as those who know more and more about less and less. For its selected functions and specific purposes, a given extension may provide a welcome enhancement of power, but the benefit might come at a high price due to the single dimensionality of that wonderful creation and the resultant fragmentation of functions.

Think, for example, of some of our public restrooms that are furnished with many items of state-of-art equipment. There may be water faucets that will shut themselves off after a certain amount of time, or that pre-mix hot and cold water to give an outflow at a controlled temperature. They are convenient and economical —except when, for instance, one is hurt and needs to run a large amount of cold water quickly on the bruise so as to curtail a swelling, or when a spill requires a rapid dousing of the spot with a flow of lukewarm water for the prevention of permanent staining.

Similarly, in such bathrooms, there may be automatic hand dryers, which the manufacturers tout as serving to save trees, reduce paper litter, and minimize the danger of disease transmission via towels. This sounds wonderful, but wait until you accidentally cut yourself, upset a glass of drink, or are faced with your baby's "accident." Then, you will naturally try to find something absorbent in the high-tech environment. A rather desperate solution may be to appropriate a roll of toilet tissues, but the thin, soft paper cannot retain as much moisture as paper or cloth towels, which have been supplanted by the warm air dryers. Thus, in such a situation, what is good for geese is not so good for ganders. That is exactly the trouble with focusing, or selective accentuation, which is for better or worse the hallmark of all cultural extensions.

Now, the *focused* attention also means a lack of attention to what has *not* been singled out for extension. Hall observes that "extensions are a special kind of amplifier, and in the process of amplification, important details are frequently left out.... Sometimes what is left out may be more important than what is amplified."[4] To characterize specialization, rather facetiously, as the process of learning more and more about less and less is also to suggest the concomitant effects of accentuation, namely, coming to know less and less about more and more! In either case, what prevails is the single dimensionality of function, making most extensions suitable for only one purpose. Granted that there are some devices that purport to be multifunctional—for example, a pocket camping knife with built-in scissors, file, can opener, bottle cap opener, saw, toothpick, and so forth. However, in most instances, such an implement proves, in each of its separate operations, less effective than a collection of single-function tools. There is indeed a good reason why many craftspeople sport a huge tool box in the back of their pick-up trucks so as to carry multitudinous tools.

The same phenomenon may be seen in the development of an ever larger variety of military weapons — for example, aircrafts — each aiming to do only a limited range of tasks well. Giant bombers cannot do the job of fast, sleek fighters, and vice versa. Moreover, neither bombers nor fighter planes can easily substitute for helicopters to carry soldiers or evacuate the wounded. Long-range radar surveillance planes, artillery spotters, drones for spying or training, and every other type of flying machine have been specifically designed to perform a single, intended function, and none is built to pursue multiple assignments.

In other words, wherever the focusing occurs, there always are the two complementary phenomena—illumination and obfuscation. Like when a searchlight is poised upon a ship or an airplane, the focal object gets clarified and detailed, even as everything else is swallowed up in the sharpened contrast of darkness, hardly seen at all. A body builder concentrates upon muscle building, toning, and posing to wow the spectators with a "perfect" body, but that does not necessarily mean a healthy body with balanced strength and coordinated function. Likewise, a beauty queen would understandably focus upon what shows on the outside, while her inside may be left unexplored and underdeveloped by herself, or unseen and unappreciated by others. The so-called idiot savant, a person suffering from a particular variety of autism, shows a similar juxtaposition of retaining a lot of rather useless facts and details in mind but remaining blank on other, more significant matters, or being unable to organize all the bits of information into a coherent structure.

A more subtle example is given by a person who, during and after the Second World War, had a remarkable poly-lingual experience in Europe as a high-level linguist and interpreter-negotiator. He makes the following observation of interest.

> In fact, in a curious way knowledge of a foreign language tends to inhibit one from reading widely. While the linguist is able to read the original text he often can do so only with the greatest difficulty. The ability coupled with the difficulty acts as a double deterrent: it rules out reading the work in translation and discourages struggling with the original text.[5]

This candid recognition points out the dilemma of specialized knowledge acting as a curious sort of barrier rather than as an open gate to wider, deeper, and more general linguistic involvements.

Externalization

Another peculiar feature of extension is that the more we depend upon it, the more we lose our own organismic capacity through disuse. Somewhat like the atrophying of limbs in long bedridden patients, the power originally within the person is relinquished when consigned to an extension, even as that power itself gets enhanced.

For instance, how many of us have come to depend so routinely upon a tiny calculator in balancing checkbooks or completing tax returns so as to find the rote or hand calculation increasingly more difficult? Without the confirmation given by the machine, we tend to be far less confident of the results than before. How many people can still figure out with ease and self-assurance the square root of any given number without the help of a calculator? Likewise, how many, especially amongst the younger folks of today, can correctly spell words on their own, and facilely write long, complex sentences for meaningful compositions and communications, without falling back upon some computer softwares? How many of us can still create and tell an imaginative tale to children or evocatively read and enact a story, rather than letting the movies, videos, or television serve as an alleged surrogate?

In some ways our mind seems to work much like the proverbial *tabula rasa*. Think of traditional school examinations. In preparation, the student writes a lot of things on that clean slate and carries it into the classroom. When the questions are handed out, she or he transcribes as much of that memorized information onto the pages of the "blue book." Curiously, however, once so committed onto the external paper, the information itself seems to vanish from the slate, and the learner typically remembers little. This experience is just another example of what I am calling the *externalization effects* of extension.

Needless to say, a complete erasure of memory may not in fact take place, but there is no denying that an externalization distances a person from what originated and resided within him or her. Many a writer has commented upon the peculiar experience of relating to what one thought, wrote, and published as if the ideas and phrases now belonged to somebody else. For instance, Anne Truitt remarked:

> When my work began to go out into the world in the 1960s, I found that the things I made sometimes evolved a history all their own.... as if [they] had in some authoritative way made [themselves].... [For example,] when [some years later] I saw *Spume*, which is ten feet tall, looming over me once again, I felt stunned—as if confronted by something made by someone else.[6]

This sense of "otherness" is repeatedly expressed by creators in relationship to what they themselves created. Call it objectification, detachment, or even alienation, the fact remains that, once let go, our creations are inclined to take on their own shapes, colors, and existence, while not ceasing to affect us. Here, a parallel with the experience of procreation, followed by the little person's individuation, appears rather close. As poetically put by Kahlil Gibran, "Your children are not your children.... They come through you but not from you.... You are the bows from which your children as living arrows are sent forth...."[6]

As we create, meanwhile, the *how* of creation is likely to leave indelible marks on the externalized results. Thus,

> It may well be true that the tool, the means, affects the very nature of the product,

the artistic end.... Instant technology, desktop publishing, has now made it possible to produce a book as first draft in place of a handwritten manuscript, which displayed all the paths not taken, the rejected clauses, the scratched-out word.... The apparent perfection of the printed and bound first draft may be convincing evidence to the writer of the perfection of the rough copy.... Nothing more appears to need doing. It is at the same time the first draft and the finished copy.[8]

This attitude of "once suffices" is also prevalent in much of the e-mail communication, wherein the sloppiness is excused in the name of speed and ease. It nevertheless deprives the writer of further opportunities to relate anew to what has become too close and familiar, hence taken for granted and ignored. It has often been noted that the interplay of "a passionate interest... and a certain detachment" is demanded in any truly creative work. In other words, creators show certain "detached devotion,"[9] which permits their creations "to develop its own being, its own autonomy ...out there" while allowing themselves "freedom to be dominated by the object" [or work] so created.[10] For that constructive process to take place, the creator must continue to be involved in the paradoxical engagement. If simply externalized to be forgotten or merely used for convenience, the developed means will usurp the originating power of the creator. Then, the intended empowerment through extension may ironically lead to an abatement of the very source of power.

Here is a personal example of the externalization effects, though definitely not of the "creative" variety. Some years back, when I was going on a rather extended assignment overseas, I decided to invest in a newfangled, digital wristwatch with much memory capacity. My reasoning was that, since I will have enough other things on my mind, I should not tax myself with the chore of memorizing many details, or suffer the inconvenience of carrying everywhere, all the time, a black book full of mundane information. So, I went ahead to put in the watch's memory my passport number, social security number, travellers check numbers, lock combinations, and so on and so forth, as well as the addresses and phone numbers of my friends, relatives, and other significant contacts.

Everything went well with my mission, and I congratulated myself for the wise decision to keep all such information at my fingertips without burdening my own brains. Soon after my return to the U.S. soil, I needed to have a personal cheque of a sizeable amount cashed at an out-of-state bank. As a security check, the teller requested to see my driver's license, then proceeded to ask my home phone number as a matter of routine. To my horror, I could not remember the old number which I had not had to use during my tenure out of the country. Obviously, my stumbling about triggered her suspicion, and she followed up with a question about my social security number. Alas, the same story was repeated here, since that was not an item that served any useful purpose in the particular society abroad.

In the predicament, I, at least, remembered that help was right there in my wristwatch. "Oh, just a minute, please!," said I. "You see, I carry all that sort of thing in here, *not in my head.*" I then started fumbling with the six buttons on my magic machine but, alas, it was obviously too late to convince the ever proper bank personnel. When I finally looked up to provide the *right* answer magically taken out of the watch, I found not only the alert teller in front of me, but also her supervisor as well as a burly security officer, all staring at me with an expression of utmost mistrust and hostility. "So, whose social security and phone numbers is this fellow pulling out of that machine now?" said their expressions!

I would not have made a successful criminal even if I had tried, but I could not have spoken truer words when I said, "not in my head." Whatever I had transferred into the marvellous gadget was no longer available to me since my own brains did not have to retain it at ready. My embarrassment at the bank had been bad enough, but insult was added to the injury a couple of days later when every bit of the precious stock of information in the wristwatch simply vanished when the tiny battery went dead. At that most inopportune moment, both my own brains and the tiny watch screen were utterly blank! Not only was the mighty extension useless, but it also robbed me of my original memory capacity.

To recapitulate, when not continuously exercised and actively applied, our knowledge, skills, and even emotions are inclined to atrophy and dissipate. The locus of power shifts from us to our creations, and we can continue to function *only with* the vicarious power of these tools. The more powerful the trusted extensions are, the more complete our dependence on them and the more pronounced the degeneration of our original capability. In that, Stravinsky was right: "Our mind, as well as our body, requires continual exercise. It atrophies if we do not cultivate it."[11]

De-contextualization

If the externalization effects, or the phenomenon of functional relinquishment, might be summed up as a case of *dis*placement of our original powers, we can also speak of cases of *mis*placement. These happen when the specific context, in which the augmented power was achieved through an extension, has been forgotten or ignored. What is involved in that instance is the indiscriminate application of a given extension in inappropriate settings and/or for improper purposes. One may then speak of the *de-contextualization effects* of extension.

Some misuses of the equalizing and compensating potential of extensions were already mentioned in passing in Chapter 2—a coward turning into a braggart, bully, or even a vicious killer on the strength of a knife or a gun. Similarly, a weakling may become a vindictive despot when armed with the authority of an office or a rank.

Less obvious than such sorry demonstrations of human frailty is the out-of-context application of extensions, particularly those of the nonmaterial variety. Ideas quite relevant and useful in one realm of life are often improperly used in another realm, regardless of their actual suitability. For instance, theories stemming from a particular discipline or setting have often been invoked quite *literally* to describe and make sense of experiences in other settings or disciplines. Some of the ideas in quantum physics may be cited as a case in point—the explicative formulations that, to most of us, remain mysterious but powerful, hence alluring.

For example, Truitt refers in her memoir to her twin younger sisters to make the point that "each child grows up in a singular psychological world." That is true enough, but her explanation appears a little farfetched:

> This [18-month] gap in time combines with dissimilarities in temperament to make their view of our childhood different from mine. Heisenberg's uncertainty principle—the principle that "uncertainties at the instant of measurement ... prevent complete certainty about the future course of a system under observation"—governs families as well as observable quantities in general.[12]

This particular version of Heisenberg's principle, referenced by Truitt to a large encyclopedia of science and technology, may not have been the clearest one to use, even if relevant to her intended point. A more understandable rendition says: "It is important to note that the uncertainty principle does not set limits to the precision with which either the position alone or the momentum alone [of a moving particle such as an electron in an atom] may be determined. But it does show that there is an ultimate limit to the precision with which *both* may be determined simultaneously."[13]

In any case, "many concepts of the new physics unfortunately can be formulated correctly only in the esoteric jargon of scientific discourse, or better, in abstract mathematical symbols. When these matters are discussed outside of the purlieus of professional science, it is difficult to avoid common similes and words, which can easily be misleading."[14] Meanwhile, Heisenberg himself recorded "a serious warning against the somewhat forced application of the concepts in domains where they did not belong." [15] Granted the potentially *metaphorical* power of such application, people are wont to forget the analogical, not literal, nature of this sort of overgeneralization. [See Chapter 6 for a fuller discussion of the nature and uses of such extensions as abstractions and analogies.]

Yet another example of the out-of-context application of a given idea may be found in the study of the so-called national character. Spearheaded in the 1930s by cultural anthropologists such as Ruth Benedict, Margaret Mead, and Geoffrey Gorer, the attempts were aimed at deducing the salient characteristics of an entire nation, often on the basis of observations of the folklores, shared habits, childrearing practices, and so forth, and of their psychological interpretations.[16]

While ambitious and certainly fascinating, the results have not been entirely convincing. For instance, by Gorer's own admission in 1961, his 1949 analysis of the character of the whole Russian people "attained a certain notoriety ...because of its introduction of the swaddling hypothesis and because of the wide-spread imputation that I affirmed that swaddling was 'the cause' of the Great Russian character...."[17] In rebuffing this imputation by "naive confusion," which Gorer himself admitted to be "somewhat to blame," he referred to an article written by Mead in 1954.[18] In that analysis of the reception of the swaddling hypothesis, she had reminded readers that, "A description of the process by which individuals learn is not a history of the origins of what is learned."[19] In other words, *how* people learn does not describe or explain *what* they have come to learn. Though hard to refute in itself, this statement does little to elucidate the pitfalls of decontextualization.

Alex Inkeles pointed out the common danger in the following words.

> In short, investigators sometimes reason by analogy from a (demonstrated or assumed) personality mode to the structural pattern of institutions, and posit an overly simple causal relationship.[20]

Even Gregory Bateson, another early proponent of the notion of national character, had to acknowledge that the complexity necessarily involved in its inquiry "stringently limit the scope of this concept."[21]

As regards the prevalent temptation to trace adult characters to very early experiences in life, typically along the lines of psychoanalytic reasoning, Gordon Allport had this to say.

> Recent researches have, indeed, indicated the importance of early years in the formation of character.... While Freudian and Rankian theories undoubtedly contain valuable truths, I venture to believe that they contain no more truth than certain opposing theories—those which maintain that personality is subject to constructive influences all through life; that it possesses inherent resources for growth and change at every period; and that no character is conclusively set at the age of three, or thirteen, or thirty.[22]

Finally, David Riesman adds the following reminder.

> Easy assumptions of the fixity of national character contradict the evidence of human plasticity provided by studies of acculturation, and the history of [some] societies such as the English or Swedish reminds us that peoples now well known for stability and law-abidingness were in the eighteenth century a valiantly disorderly people.... It must be repeated that behavior and proclaimed values give only inferential clues as to character structure, either in individuals or in social groups.[23]

In spite of the ever present risk of overgeneralization, application of a theory out of its original context is quite widespread. Granted that the practice sometimes leads to salutary crossbreeding of ideas, a faddish borrowing from currently popular interpretations is more likely to bring forth misguided efforts and misleading arguments. For example, Augustin Berque refers to one such instance in which semiotic and hermeneutic approaches [after, say, Roland Barthes and Jacques Derrida] were applied in the study of the architectural-geographical features of Japanese cities. The "grammar" of, for instance, Tokyo was examined as if its street were a phrase and the city itself were a text. Berque proceeded to point out the errors in this endeavor of literally transposing a method of analysis from one domain to another and of thereby reducing the multidimensional place of human encounters to a mere system of signs or a bookful of symbols.[24]

Let me add just one more example of de-contextualization and over-generalization. In 1972, a research paper on the maternal attachment of the newborns appeared in a prestigious medical journal.[25] Four years later, on the basis of that research, an influential book, called *Maternal-Infant Bonding*, was published.[26] During the following decade, "bonding" had become a household word, and the then prevailing obstetric routine of separating the newborn from the mother very soon after birth for half a day or longer came under attack as a contributing factor to subsequent attachment failure and other developmental difficulties, and even child abuse. The presumed imperative for mother-baby bonding triggered changes in health care practice so as to allow [and, in fact, insist upon] an immediate and continued postpartum physical contact between the new mother and her baby.

In fact, the whole notion of bonding had originated in studies of such animals as rats and goats wherein an after-birth separation was seen to be associated with maternal rejection of the offspring. That sort of observation fit in with the idea of the "critical periods"—certain times in the life course when an organism must undergo some particular experiences if it were to continue developing normally. For instance, the "imprinting" of the mother-following behavior in some birds must take place during the first few days. Once that has been accomplished, the baby birds will follow *that* mother and only her, even if the *mother* happens to be Professor Konrad Lorenz![27] On the other hand, the absence of the essential experiences during these important junctures are believed to result in arrestment of development and irreparable damage.

Amongst the species of *Homo sapiens,* however, any specific, in-born critical periods have never been clearly established, even though the general importance of early childhood experience is by now widely acknowledged. [See Chapter 1 for a related discussion.] The original "bonding" studies themselves, which claimed to have found such a period at the immediate postpartum juncture, has since been severely challenged by many researchers.[28] The general conclusion from such critical assessments of the research evidence is that, while mother-infant attachment is important, there is little support for the existence of early bonding in humans.[29] Following her extensive review and analysis two decades after the onset of the bonding fever, Eyer declares that "the investigation of bonding was distorted by the overwhelming need to reform childbirth and by the overpowering assumptions people have about instincts, the proper role of women, and the infinite malleability of infants," and decries the widespread feelings of guilt and anguish created among many new mothers, natural or adoptive, who could not or did not bond at birth, by the "overstated imperatives that prove to be groundless."[30]

Many other instances of de-contextualization can be readily cited, especially in social and human sciences, where the operational boundaries of a given theory are seldom clearly spelled out. It is not that the borrowing of ideas from different theories would not sometimes open up a new vista and bring a rich cross-fertilization among different realms of understanding. Rather, it is that the instances of misapplication typically reflect a naïve and dogmatic insistence on the total inclusiveness, know-it-all-ness, of a particular idea, approach, or theoretical formulation, which betrays an unawareness of the appropriate context, ignores the proper limits of relevance, and stifles other considerations and possibilities.

After all, something must have gone awry somewhere when people are convinced that there is a very simple solution to all the ills of, for instance, public schooling, and adamantly advise a wholesale transfer of the business ideology and modus operandi to education. Similarly, one must be more than a little skeptical where most everyone eagerly confesses that her or his family of orientation was prototypically "dysfunctional," wherein all the members were inescapably "codependent"! Yet, it remains quite a challenge to recognize the proper contextual limits for any prevailing interpretations and contentions.

To summarize, the misapplication of extensional power through de-contextualization results from the difficulty in being aware of the original circumstances under which a particular extension was developed for certain specific purposes. It is often hard to tell when and where we are crossing the proper boundaries of application. Thus, we unwarily step into foreign territories, still believing our charts and courses to be correct and true, and often wander in the harm's way.

Spillover

Speaking of boundaries, it is worth noting that therapists and counselors often mention the "boundary problems" from which some of their clients suffer. What is being talked about is the kind of difficulties people run into in the absence of a clear sense of personal boundaries, i.e., where one as a person begins and ends, both in terms of the consciousness of the body limits and in relation to the sense of self or personhood.

It needs to be recognized, first of all, that personal boundaries do not coincide with our spatial body limits and cannot be defined "in terms of the actual amount of air displaced by [the] body [since] man has around him as extensions of his personality the zones," starting at the "intimate distance" and successively expanding into the "personal distance," "social distance," and "public distance"[31] The actual shape and size of such "spatial envelopes" differ from culture to culture, and also vary from individual to individual even within a given culture. Early on, children learn without explicit explanation and instruction where and how close they may, and should, position themselves in relation to other people for different interactions—when being fed, cuddling up, playing, conversing, fighting, talking to a group, engaging in transactions, and so on and so forth. They will continue, as adults, to conduct themselves, still mostly unawares, within the boundaries their culture implicitly stipulates as proper. These "informal [i.e., unstated] spatial patterns have distinct bounds, and such deep, if unvoiced, significance that they form an essential part of the culture. To misunderstand this significance may invite disaster."[32]

Needless to say, the potential disaster is not limited to intercultural contacts. Within a given culture, one's sense of identity is closely related to that of privacy, and a person can feel harassed and violated when somebody else encroaches upon his or her individual boundaries. For instance, the very first U.S. court case was heard in 1994 over the "electronic stalking" of a person (a woman in the particular situation) by another (a man) via the e-mail, phone, and regular mail. "Although she was never physically approached or threatened by [the man], the woman pressed charges under Michigan law, which requires only that the target of unwanted attention be frightened or intimidated, or feel harassed or threatened, by repeated contacts, whether physical or electronically.... The ...case highlights the new legal challenges, and potential for abuse, posed by the growing popularity of electronic communications."[33]

Of course, the medium of interaction is not the critical issue here. The crux of the matter is, rather, the collective definition and individual perception of *personal* boundary. "Suppose I am a blind man, and I use a stick," asks Bateson. "Where do *I* start?"[34] Likewise, where does his *I* end? In a similar vein, how far do, and should, differing countries' coastal waters extend, and where are the international waters to begin for open fishing or oil prospecting? Regardless of the definition or proclamation, when one crosses over boundaries into somebody else's territory, trouble begins.

Furthermore, such boundaries do not have to be between different individuals or peoples. They can be located within the same person. For example, the "Parent, Adult, and Child" within an individual Ego have been described by Eric Berne as "the phenomenological realities."[35]

The Parent is the guide for ethical aspirations...; the Adult is concerned with the earthly realities of objective living; and the Child is a purgatory, and sometimes a hell, for archaic tendencies.... Ego boundaries appear to function like complex membranes of highly selective permeability. Lesions of the boundary between the Adult and the Child may give rise to any of the special group of symptoms which may be called "boundary symptoms": feelings of unreality, estrangement, depersonalization, jamais vu, déja vu, and their analogues, such as the well-known déja raconté.[36]

This whole phenomenon, wherein boundary confusion and encroachment bring negative consequences, may be called the *spill-over effects* of extensions. The analogy is to a reservoir created by damming a river—a body of water usable for many purposes including the drinking water, irrigation, recreation, fish hatchery, and hydroelectric power. However, all these benefits hinge upon the intactness of the dam and reservoir. If and when the water overflows the reservoir boundaries, or the dam breaks, there is bound to be considerable damages. Similarly, cultural extensions can be quite powerful and useful *within* their intended realm of application. Beyond the proper limits of operation, however, they may inflict unplanned or unknown harm. Such clearly negative consequences wrought beyond the boundaries justify the separate label of the spillover effects, distinguishing them from the de-contextualization effects examined above.

We can find an example of the spillover effects in the national obsession with psychological testing. In John Gardner's words,

> Of all mistakes made in using aptitude tests, perhaps the worst are made in trying to apply the results beyond the strictly academic or intellectual performances for which the tests were designed.... This error produces a grievous difficulties when we try to identify young people who will exhibit high performance in later life. Performance in later life places rather heavy emphasis on precisely those attributes not measured by scholastic aptitude and achievement tests—zeal, character, judgment, staying power, and so on.... The tests were not designed to test success in life.[38]

In spite of this apt reminder, schools continue to use the scores on the so-called objective tests of achievement as the ultimate criterion for their performance as an institution. Thus, we see every three or four months the average test scores for each school as well as for each district published in newspapers and other mass media. The accompanying comments equate the ups and downs of such figures with the success or failure in the schooling of youngsters. Needless to say, individual students' scores are interpreted in a like manner as a sure measure of not merely their past attainment but also their future potential.

The irony of it is that, even as American society is thus quite keen on differentiating people in terms of their alleged promises, it also reveals extreme *"equalitarianism wrongly conceived,"* which can ultimately bring forth "a rejection of all standards and tolerance of mediocrity and shabbiness in every aspect of our national life. We have seen mediocrity breed mediocrity."[39]

Echoing this assessment, May Sarton noted the following in one of her journals.

> If there are to be no distinctions between people, if achievement or simply a great wholeness of being ... is meaningless, since "we are all equal," then what is life about? ... And for that reason it is a little too easy for someone who has not spent years and years trying to write well and has not achieved even a very

little to say "We are equals, you and I," to a writer who has achieved something in a long life, and for someone of forty to say to someone of seventy "We are exactly alike" is ludicrous and an underestimation of what life itself does to force us to maturity.[40]

Our society has also suffered from the spillover effects of the "radical individualism." While the culture claims to honor each person's independence, the expectation that everyone must be individually strong enough, smart enough, and resourceful enough all the time everywhere has done much to the undervaluing of the necessity of interdependence in many realms of life. The familiar declaration, "I can take care of myself!" reflects as much haughtiness and contrariness as reasonable self-confidence. "It is," observed Marian Wright Edelman, "a dangerously short-sighted nation that fantasizes absolute self-sufficiency as the only correct way of life."[41]

Among both individuals and families, this expectation of self-sufficiency has served to isolate many who are unable, for whatever reasons, to look after themselves unassisted. Thus, for instance, Leontine Young noted that abusing and neglecting families share one important tendency: "they do not ask for help with their family problems."[42] In turn, the larger society has often reacted with a social distancing from, and condemnation of, those who appear unable to live up to the canon of independence. "This isolation is dangerous," says Young. "It is dangerous for society and for both the parents and children of these families."[43] Edelman, too, points to the danger of "the peculiarly American amnesia or hypocrisy that wants us to think that poor and middle-class families must fend entirely for themselves."[44]

In fact, "the discovery of the individual, the creation or invention of 'modern man,' was also paradoxically the source of the first portent of alienation...."[45] In the extreme form of individualism, the "me-first" attitude, which is the hallmark of narcissism,[46] leads to action aimed strictly for personal gains, and "the conception of broader, public good recedes from view."[47] What is being lost in this self-centered quest is not merely the "communal existence as a meaning larger than that of the individual...,"[48] but also the sense of the personal self itself.

This is because "the fundamental fact of human existence is man with man."[49] As observed by Fromm:

Unless [a person] belonged somewhere.... he would not be able to relate himself to any system which would give meaning and direction to his life, he would be filled with doubt, and his doubt eventually would paralyze his ability to act— that is to live.[50]

Perhaps predictably, the spirit of radical individualism seems to have spilled over elsewhere. How we *do* science is a case in point. As noted by Stephen Toulmin,

Every independent scientific discipline is marked by its own specialized modes of abstraction; and the issues to be considered in each discipline are so defined that they can be investigated and discussed independently of—in abstraction from—issues belonging to other disciplines.[51]

A related example may be found in the increasing dysfunctionality of the liberal/general education curriculum in our colleges and universities. "The triumph of the academic department as an autonomous unit capable of demanding greater loyalty than the institution of which it is a part is certainly the primary cause of the splintering of the liberal arts curriculum that we see all around us today."[52] Thus, "the typical curriculum focus[es] predominantly on the subject matter of various disciplines, with little or no thought given to relationships *among* bodies of knowledge."[53] What prevails is a culture of division and separation , rather than one of integration and coherence.

Needless to say, harmful spillovers are not limited to the realm of nonmaterial extensions. For instance, in hot summer evenings, when I am pestered by a swarm of mosquitoes, I certainly feel like picking up some such powerful weapons as the bazooka to attack and annihilate the unwelcome intruders. Of course, if I indeed followed up on my urge, I would be witnessing the full extent of the spillover effects, wherein an extensive damage is inflicted upon many properties and people with little impact upon the targeted insects themselves.

To take another example, our well-meant humanitarian actions have frequently backfired to our surprise and dismay. Many CARE packages were sent to areas ravaged by wars or natural disasters of one sort or another. For a period, a large quantity of powdered milk, among others, was shipped overseas in the hope of helping, in particular, starving children. Unfortunately, the efforts turned out to be yet another case of "the best laid schemes o' mice and men [that] gang aft a-glley."[54] In Asia, the product based on cow's milk made many babies sick, since certain enzymes needed to digest it were absent in their bodies due to their customary diet. In Africa, on the other hand, the difficulty was not with the substance per se, but lay in the frequently contaminated water used to liquefy the powdered milk. As a result, what had been believed to be a universal nutrient proved useless at best, and injurious at worst.

Somewhat parallel to this example was my experience following another overseas assignment. I had come home with a certain troublesome condition in my digestive system, and went to see a generalist first, then a specialist in internal medicine. In spite of the powerful antibiotics prescribed to remove the suspected parasites, my health continued to worsen. A different antibiotic medication was given by another specialist, while a fiber-optic intestinal examination was conducted by a third specialist. Still, there was no improvement. In exasperation, I turned to yet another doctor who, while traditional in the main, also practiced homeopathy where relevant. Her assessment was that all the potent drugs had in fact been quite effective in removing the parasites themselves. The trouble was that, in that curative process, these same agents managed to kill off other microorganisms that keep my digestive system functional. Apparently, the typical allopathic approach directly aimed at the source of the ill spilled over to cause an extensive damage to the broader base of my health.

Still other cases of spillovers may be seen in the uses of two substances, DDT and asbestos. The DDT (*d*ichloro*d*iphenyl-*t*richloroethane) is a powerful insecticide that served to save many lives during and after the Second World War by staving off the potential epidemic ravages carried by, among others, lice. The asbestos is any of the mineral forms of magnesium silicate that separate into long, threadlike fibers. Known since the Greco-Roman times, it does not burn, is resistant to chemicals, and does not conduct heat or electricity. Understandably, it has been quite useful in building insulation, fireproofing, and other applications. Both these materials are thus very convenient and effective for their respective, specific purposes, and they had been widely utilized. Unfortunately, more recent experiences have shown both to be carcinogenic (i.e., cancer-causing), and that destructive spillover effect has since led to a severe restriction of their routine usage.

To recapitulate, the spillover effects refer here to the harmful consequences of the power of extensions over and beyond their intended, appropriate boundaries. Even though such misapplication is frequently made unawares, the negative results are more direct and concrete than in many cases of de-contextualization. Such double-edged character of extension may remind one of the warning that, "All they that take the sword shall perish with the sword."[55]

Extension Transference

Powerful they certainly are but, as noted repeatedly, that very power of cultural extensions can work against us. The most far-reaching of the negative consequences may be summarized under the caption of the "extension transference." Hall described the process this way:

> The principle of extension transference ... holds that any extension not only can but usually does eventually take the place of the process which has been extended.... [That is to say,] whenever something is extended, the extension begins to take on a life of its own and quickly becomes confused with the reality it replaces.[56]

In practically every case of transference, therefore, the extension as such becomes mistaken for the process or function extended so as to be falsely ascribed the properties and powers it does *not* in fact possess. A familiar example of this confusion is seen in the making and worshiping of icons and idols in spite of the explicit prohibitions of such practice in the teachings of most major religions. The ineffable encounter with some being or reality far broader, deeper, and complex than ourselves would be abstracted into a shorthand like "God," "the Holy," "the Almighty," "the Eternal," or "Nirvana," and thereafter the name itself is invoked for the sense of overwhelming power and glory. Statues, paintings, and myriad other "sacred" artifacts are created to be cherished, adorned, adored, guarded, and worshipped for potentially inducing the original oceanic feelings of awe, wonder, reverence, transcendence, and unification. The power is thus arrogated to *our* creations and, thenceforth, we live under the spell of such extensions.

When we look at how this transference process applies in our daily life, several phases of progression may be identified.

The first phase of transference. At the outset, we come to know and judge others *by* extensions they possess and use. An episode written by a sports journalist can illustrate this initial phase. In a book of touching reminiscences about the life and death (by Lou Gehrig's disease) of his teacher, Prof. Morris Schwartz of Brandeis University, Mitch Albom reported the following.

> In March of 1995, a limousine carrying Ted Koppel, the host of ABC-TV's "Nightline," pulled up to the ... curb outside Morrie's house.... Several of Morrie's friends and family members had gathered to meet Koppel, and when the famous man entered the house, they buzzed with excitement—all except Morrie.[57]

The easy association of the big limousine with the power and status of its occupant is the crux of the first phase of transference. If a person drives a Rolls-Royce, Jaguar, Mercedes-Benz, or Alpha Romeo, rather than a Ford, Chevrolet, or Huyndai, or better yet, if she or he is being chauffeured around in such a car, that person must *obviously* be important. He or she must own a huge property with a big house or two, each with many bedrooms and bathrooms and a multiple car garage. The person is *evidently* quite successful—even though all the land possessions may actually fall in the category of the proverbial one of "the cheapest in the richest neighborhood." Similarly, if she or he carries, either preceding or following her or his name, some titles (like Doctor, Reverend, President, Executive Director, Attorney-at-Law), degrees (e.g., L.L.D., M.D., M.B.A., D.D., and Ph.D.), and organizational acronyms (e.g., AIA, UPTA, ASMS, or even some concocted ones!), that person must be definitely brighter and more competent than the rest of us.

Whether we acknowledge it or not, all of us evaluate and infer each other's worth in terms of the extensions on display and in use – what does the party wear (a custom-made dress? a silk suit? a French handbag? Italian shoes? a Rolex? or a *mere* Timex?!) and reveal (in the language, social decorum and manners; conversational topics; school names; job titles; favorite newspapers, magazines, and books; locales of residence; preferred varieties of food, drinks, music, arts, leisure activities, etc.; vacation spots and durations; names of friends and acquaintances; and so on). These snippets powerfully control our first impressions and, alas, the extension transference has led many of us astray at the hand of shrewd confidence men and women in many walks of life.

The second phase. Even more unfortunately, in the second phase of transference, the same approach is followed for our self-assessment. In other words, we evaluate and judge ourselves in relationship to the extensions we possess and use. For example, a middle age woman begins her painful, plodding autobiography by referring to "a New York apartment which isn't" hers. At age 37, she says, "I don't have a life, I'm just using up a number of days somehow.... No obligation to anyone requires me to live in this apartment, or in this city." While she has had "a trail of men," she is not married. Although she has a doctorate in philosophy from one of the most prestigious universities in America, she is "not teaching at a good college" and not even regularly. Needless to say, she feels hard pressed: "I have no money.... I always say I have no money." By her own admission, she has no established domicile of her own, no man, no steady job, and no money—indeed not much to show in terms of accepted and acceptable extensions. "I don't live anywhere; I perch."[58] Predictably, it takes a long, hard struggle before she gets away from the second phase of transference.

Again, we must face the fact that it is so easy for all of us to judge our own value by the comparative accumulations of extensions. Suppose that our family managed to take only one vacation trip last year, while our neighbors took three. Accordingly, we *are* inferior. Or, let us say that I had meant to earn a doctorate and publish an influential book before I turn 30. In fact, I may have only managed to get a Bachelor's degree by that age, and no book of any sort is in sight at 48. *Hence,* I am a dunce. Or, suppose yet again that my little sister is a vice president in a Fortune 200 company, earning more than $280,000 a year, in contrast to poor me who is a mere foreman in a small factory, barely making $35,000 with overtime. *Obviously,* I am a failure. To think, feel, and act thus—mistaking the power and the market value of the "tools" (extensions) at our disposal for the inherent worth and meaning of ourselves as persons— leads to the denigration of life and dignity.

The third phase. The affront becomes quite clear in the next progression in transference. In the first two phases, other people or we ourselves were defined *by* extensions. Now, in this third phase, people are defined *as* extensions. That is to say, we start treating others as if they were extensions, and end up using them as our tools for attaining our goals. For instance, I may be quite eager to become your "friend," but I will remain your friend *only so long as* you are useful for my purposes with what you happen to have—your looks, youth, money, status, connections, or any other features and possessions helpful for my self-promotion and -aggrandizement. Accordingly, you cannot expect to see me hanging around once your value *to me* has been exhausted. You then become a handicap to me, an embarrassment and a burden rather than an asset, ceasing to be a convenient and useful means to my end. My so-called friendship has little to do with such "sentimentality" as affection, respect, or loyalty. It is, instead, a purely utilitarian arrangement of convenience.

Sadly, we can readily see examples of such ruthlessly exploitative orientation in many social relationships. Slavery is a historic case in point, wherein people were literally made into properties and the source of energy (i.e., the manpower). A similar perspective was reflected in the title of a Canadian television program, "Anybody's Son Will Do." It looked at the handling of the national need for expendable personnel in the military.[58] Additional examples of the notorious penchant for expediency, manipulation, and exploitation are abundant in politics everywhere.

In yet another realm, even a captain of industry may realize, especially at the point of retirement, that he or she is quite disposable and replaceable, typically with little appreciation for the hard-earned experience and expertise. Thus, a former chief executive officer of several conglomerates is quoted admitting that "when you suddenly leave the [corporate] jungle, life is pretty empty ... The phone stops ringing. You start wanting to have lunch with old friends ... but they're busy, they are working. They've got a job to do and just don't have the time to talk to anybody where it doesn't involve their business.... I am not in demand anymore, I'm seeking company rather than being sought."[60]

Closer home, some of the allegedly intimate relationships betray the same, calculating character of transaction in which love is at best conditional, and commitment typically remains transitory. The manipulative motives and dynamics of the fake "friendship," mentioned earlier, may apply equally to the interactions between lovers, spouses, or "partners." Many people have suffered from a highly destructive experience of abuse, often repeatedly. Reports have not been rare of those who romanced and married certain target persons for money, promotion, emigration, or espionage. Even more sobering are the stories of devastating exploitation of the young and, increasingly, the old within the family context. In all these sorry instances, one realizes that the third phase of extension transference creates injustice "in which a man is not an end in himself, but becomes a means for the ends of another man."[61]

Children have frequently become the means for grownups' ends, the economic (e.g., child labor) and sexual exploitation being two of the most blatant examples.[62] However, less extreme forms of manipulation within the family contexts can still hold seeds of destruction. The young caught in ugly custody fights, or the aged targeted for greedy inheritance disputes, are pawns for machinations. Likewise, children forced to assume such premature roles as family mediator, decision maker, and counselor typically suffer from the experience of "being a means for the end of another." For example, in detailed post-suicide reflections upon an adolescent, a therapist and a teacher noted that, "Her sense of justice and fair play led Vivienne [the young girl] to be used sometimes to settle family disputes ... Vivienne was the mediator."[63] Indeed, a letter sent by the girl, who took her own life at the age of 14, to another teacher whom she had adored corroborates the untenable position in which she was finding herself: "Mommy came to me for help. And I really have helped her whenever I could. But it puts a certain pressure on me; I'm not even fourteen yet, and Mommy's forty-eight."[64]

There are even more subtle forms of manipulation in daily interactions, which are not necessarily guided by any malicious intentions on the part of the parents. For instance, David Elkind suspects "a strong tie between parental job dissatisfaction, on the one hand, and a disproportionate concern with offspring's success in sports, on the other." Adult pressure for the child's early accomplishments in music, dance, gymnastics, beauty contest, drama, and other activities often "reflects parental need, not the child's need or inclination," so as to bolster the parents' "self-esteem with a precocious son or daughter."[65]

Similarly, a child, especially a bright one, might indeed serve as a "status symbol" for the middle-class, stay home mothers who are "often regarded as unambitious (and therefore less intelligent than [their] working counterparts) and generally lacking in self-respect and female pride."[66] That could be so but, to be fair, it must also be pointed out that a childbirth or an adoption may be serving the same function for many a professional woman of middle class who longs, no matter how covertly, to prove to herself and others that she is truly a "Superwoman," successful not only as an upward mobile careerist in men's world but also as a woman, lover, wife, and mother. In either case, the proud parent may later face, to her chagrin, an unexpected protest from her prize offspring who has come to the painful "insight that all the love he has captured ... was not meant for him as he really was, that the admiration for his beauty and achievements was aimed at this beauty and these achievements, and not at the child himself."[67]

A hard lesson to learn in this connection was spelled out by Truitt in the following words.

> Unless we are very, very careful, we doom each other by holding onto images of one another based on preconception that are in turn based on indifference to what is other than ourselves. This indifference can be, in its extreme, a form of murder and seems to me a rather common phenomenon. We claim autonomy for ourselves and forget that in so doing we can fall into the tyranny of defining other people as we would like them to be. By focusing on what we choose to acknowledge in them, we impose an insidious control on them....
> The opposite of this inattention is love, is the honoring of others in a way that grants them the grace of their own autonomy and allows mutual discovery.[68]

The fourth phase. We have said that, in the third phase of extension transference, "a strong need to exploit others ... to make them of use" to oneself becomes salient. Thus, "any situation or relationship is looked at from the standpoint of 'what can I get out of it?'—whether it has to do with money, prestige, contacts, or ideas."[69] Almost predictably, then, the same attitude is shown to one's own person in the fourth phase of transference. That is to say, the exploitative orientation is directed against oneself. Just as other people were seen and used as a tool, so is the self now seen and used as a tool unto itself. A person becomes an extension to herself or himself and, at that point, the person becomes a slave to his or her pride, passion, greed, or any others of the moralists' "seven deadly sins."[70]

If this sounds improbable, simply look around at many people of ambition and drive, who relentlessly push themselves to climb the ladder of *success*, corporate, political, military, academic, religious, social, or wherever else, in their seemingly insatiable search for more fame and power, status and wealth. Or, their all-consuming quest may be for eternal youth and beauty. The paths taken may vary, but all such endeavors are essentially for the same elusive goal of finding happiness and good life, here defined in a unidimensional manner. Also shared among all these people are the driven-ness with which they use themselves as the ultimate tool.

Interestingly, some of them explicitly acknowledge themselves to be their own means, saying, for instance, "I came to the habit of using my self as a tool."[71] Most , however, are unlikely to be so aware of how they are looking at, and relating to, themselves. Meanwhile, some of the metaphors of the body, prevalent in our culture,[72] clearly reveal the underlying attitudes at this fourth level of transference. Thus, a person may be "a beast of burden" unto himself or herself, an animal to be tamed, trained, and driven for hard labor. For maximum results, maximum efforts are demanded at all times. The so-called workaholics certainly fit this pattern. The beast may lurk even in the non-work realms of life. For instance, Carol-Lynne Moore reminds us that the muscle mass, which body builders spend months and years increasing, is not really for strength but for size and shape. "Such men and women may seem to be Herculean beasts of burden. But in reality, they are animated sculptures.... The hours that body builders, dancers, and models spend gazing at themselves in mirrors, and the narcissism that results, make them objects in their own eyes as much as they are objects to us."[73]

Or, the body a person uses as her or his tool may be thought of as "a machine" rather than as a beast. Machines are strong, powerful, errorless, reliable, and neutral. Accordingly, many a person expects of self (and others) all the durability, potency, consistency, precision, and freedom from any encumbering feelings and values. The person cannot tolerate weaknesses and failures, and must always be perfect at everything undertaken. In relation to the vogue of physical fitness, Moore comments further:

> Unfortunately, whenever I observe certain people joylessly jogging or bouncing determinedly in an aerobic dance class, I cannot help wondering "fit for what?" It seems such activities are engaged in less for the intrinsic pleasure of the activity than for the by-product of cardiovascular efficiency. The dream body pursued here is not an aesthetic one, but one of mechanical efficacy.[74]

A relevant fable from Japan may be told here about a master mask maker. He had already carved many great masks for Noh plays when he managed to come up with a demon mask that impressed even himself. It was truly fearsome. While admiring his own consummate artistry, a mischievous idea came to him. With this mask, he can have lots of fun scaring village people, perhaps even some beasts. So, he put it on and went around in the dark, really frightening to death every creature he encountered. He finally came home after hours of enjoyment, and proceeded to take the mask off. Alas, mysteriously, it would not come off, no matter how hard he tried. Without his realizing it, the mask had become the master. Now, he himself was indeed the malicious, ferocious demon!

This, final phase of extension transference epitomizes "the character orientation which is rooted in the experience of oneself as a commodity and of one's value as exchange value" which Fromm called "the marketing orientation."[75] The person essentially vanishes, since "man ... becomes a means himself in the service of means."[76] In fact, the discussion in this chapter of the varieties of the potentially negative effects of extensions points to the persistent danger of human's "becoming their [i.e., extensions'] helpless accomplice and passive victim."[77]

In lieu of recapitulation, Table 3-1 lists the detrimental effects of extension.

Table 3-1. Some Detrimental Effects of Extensions

FOCUSING
EXTERNALIZATION
DECONTEXTUALIZATION
SPILLOVER
EXTENSION TRANSFERENCE

Notes

1. Shelley, 1981.
2. Hall, 1977, 48.
3. Postman, 1993, 101.
4. Hall, 1983, 120.
5. Bailey, 1974, 21-22.
6. Truitt, 1997, 157.
7. Gibran, 1963, 18-19.
8. Grumbach, 1995, 178 & 179-180.
9. Henle, 1962, 45.
10. Bruner, 1962b, 14.
11. Stravinsky, 1970, 56.
12. Truitt, 1997, 28.
13. Guillemin, 1968, 94.
14. Ibid.. 246.
15. Heisenberg, 1958, 199.
16. E.g., Gorer, 1948, 1955, 1967; Gorer and Rickman, 1949; M. Mead, 1943.
17. Gorer, 1962, xxxi.
18. M. Mead, 1954.
19. Gorer, 1962, xxxii.
20. Inkeles, 1997, 105.
21. Bateson, 1972, 94.
22. Allport, 1964, 286.
23. Riesman, 1967, 37, 46.
24. Berque, 1993, 107.
25. Klaus, Jerauld et al., 1972.
26. Klaus and Kennell, 1976.
27. Lorenz, 1952.
28. E.g., Herbert, 1983; Lamb, 1982; Leiderman, 1981; Myers, 1984.
29. Minde, 1986.
30. Eyer, 1992, 12, 13.
31. Hall, 1969, 128.
32. Ibid., 112.
33. Lewis, 1994.
34. Bateson, 1972, 459.
35. Berne, 1975, 4.
36. Ibid., 47, 51.
37. In the sense of my usage here, the effects reflect the "cost spillovers" more closely than the "benefit spillovers." See, e.g., Hirsch, 1964.
38. Gardner, 1987, 64, 65. Also see Sorokin, 1956, for a thorough, earlier criticism of the testing perspective and praxis.

39. Gardner, 1987, 30, 29.
40. Sarton, 1987, 180, 181.
41. Edelman, 1992, 90.
42. Young, 1971, 135.
43. Ibid., 133.
44. Edelman, 1992, 90-91.
45. Montagu and Matson, 1984, xx.
46. Lasch, 1979.
47. Gergen, 1991, 240.
48. Friedman, 1974, 359.
49. Buber, 1965, 203.
50. Fromm, 1965, 36.
51. Toulmin, 1982, 228.
52. Chambers, 1981, 48.
53. Riley, 1980, 299.
54. Burns, 1968, stanza 7.
55. Matt. 26:52.
56. Hall, 1983, 120, 121.
57. Albom, 1997, 18, 19.
58. Koller, 1983, 2, 1.
59. Canadian Broadcasting Corporation, 1983, 8.
60. Terkel, 1996, 9-10 & xxv.
61. Fromm, 1971, 57.
62. The United Nations "Convention on the Right of the Child," 1989, names child labor in Article 32, sex in Article 34, and all other forms of exploitation in Article 36.
63. Mack and Hickler, 1982, 17.
64. Ibid., 60.
65. Elkind, 1981, 30, 32.
66. Ibid., 36.
67. Miller, 1983, 15.
68. Truitt, 1984, 46.
69. Horney, 1966, 65.
70. Schimmel, 1997.
71. Truitt, 1997, 112.
72. Moore, 1987.
73. Moore, 1992, 363.
74. Ibid.
75. Fromm, 1967, 76.
76. Tillich, 1952, 138.
77. Mumford, 1952, 11.

Chapter 4. The Self-Portrait

The acquisition and usage of the *right kinds* of extensions, as defined by the social agreements at a particular epoch in a given culture, provide a person with much accentuated power and legitimated status.[1] Typically, as noted in the preceding chapter, such status and power are *ascribed* by others to the person and, in turn, *assumed* by the person herself or himself. Indeed, the extensions provide the social, as well as individual, definition of a person as a person.

Newly acquired wealth gives a ready illustration of this interactive dynamics. The money allows a nouveau riche to obtain *desirable* properties (e.g., land, house, furniture, clothing, automobile, yacht, or even airplane) and to follow a *desired* style of life (domestic help, elite club memberships, prestigious social parties, luxurious mode of travel, extended vacations, etc.). The accumulation and display of select material extensions are coupled with the adoption of certain nonmaterial extensions, like the idea of a good life, aspirations for respectability, and acceptable manners of behavior. The two sets of extensions complement each other. As the person is being treated as more worthy and significant than before, he or she feels more important and acts more powerful than before. Needless to say, this sequence also operates in reverse to reveal the so-called power of positive thinking.

Thus, extensions have much to do with how one relates to, and makes sense of, oneself. However, the key extension in this whole dynamics is non-material in nature. It is called the self-concept or self-image, that is to say, the idea one forms about oneself, or the picture one draws in mind of oneself. The essence of this process of idea formation or picture drawing has been aptly captured in the phrase of Charles Horton Cooley, namely, "the reflected or looking-glass self": "Each to each a looking-glass; Reflects the other that doth pass."[2]

Since none of us can directly see ourselves to figure out who we are, we must first depend upon the eyewitness reports of others to infer what we are like. It is like looking into mirrors held up by other people and coming to believe what we see therein to be what we actually are. This experience is readily seen in the very young. Babies, to begin with, do not know that they are babies—they just drink, eliminate, cry, sleep, and grow. They are meanwhile surrounded by people who look after them and respond to them. These grownups hold and carry the babies, caress and rock them, nurse and change them, sing and speak to them, play with them, bathe and clothe them, talk about them, and so forth. Each such interaction provides the babies with messages about what they are like—nice, strong, cute, bad, somebody's look-alike, or what-have-you. Early on, therefore, the babies see many images [allegedly of themselves] in the mirrors held up by different people.

Although the looking-glass analogy itself is visual, the communication is naturally through any and all media and sense modalities, and the messages so conveyed may be quite subtle. Thus, for instance, D.W. Winnicott reminded us that "the main things that a mother does with the baby cannot be [and are not] done through words. This is very obvious but it is also a very easy thing to forget." In fact, he further observed, "an infant who is held well enough is quite a different thing from one who has not been held well enough."[3] Similarly, Harry Stack Sullivan spoke of the complex dynamics of the anxiety-driven "self system," starting with babies' experience with "good, bad, and wrong nipples," which leads to the formulation of infantile notions of the "good vs. bad mother," and being followed by self-personification of "good-me, bad-me, and not-me."[4]

The point is that, as noted by George Herbert Mead, "the self ... is essentially a social structure... [and, thus,] it is impossible to conceive of a self arising outside of social experience."[5] Not surprisingly, the formation of the rudimentary picture of oneself and of the complementary picture of the surrounding world appear to begin quite early. As a matter of fact, it has been observed that "by age two, or two and a half, children are likely to give evidence of consciousness of own and others' racial characteristics," that is to say, differences in such features as the skin color, hair quality, and facial traits. Furthermore, "by the age of four ... many will have developed distinct in-group/out-group *orientations* (incipient race attitudes)."[6] In other words, there arrives a racial awareness first, closely followed by racial preferences, which tend to serve ethnocentric stereotypes and prejudices. We shall come back to further discussion of this subject in the following section, but let us first identify several basic features of the relationship between the self and the picture-in-mind of that very self.

The Self and Its Image

Enigmatically, first of all, we cannot know our self, i.e., who we are, directly and completely. Here, a distinction drawn between the two words, *I* and *me,* becomes significant. The *I* refers to the *self,* the whole person, the being that lives, loves, and labors. In other words, this is the agent who acts, reflects, and feels from birth to death. Nevertheless, there is one thing even this agent, this self, cannot do *by itself,* and that is to grasp and comprehend fully what it is.

The unknowability of the self. To accomplish the task of defining and understanding itself, the *I* must, in a manner of speaking, step out to join others as an observer and appraiser. The way this is done is to stare into the looking glasses held up by others to see what is being reflected therein. "Ah, that *must be* me!" reasons *I*. In the absence, initially at least, of any ready means of corroboration or refutation of what one is about, the *I* has to believe the image in the mirror to be itself: "Ah, that *is* me!"

The *me,* in other words, is a composite of the reflections seen in the looking glasses. If I ask someone, let us say, a woman, a question, "Who are you?" she probably begins her answer saying something like, "My name is Joycelyn Papagolas, and I am a lawyer with the Boston firm of Simpson, Sampson, and

Thompson." In our culture, such attempt at characterization may include one's name, age (especially when young), sex (though mostly obvious), place of origin, ethnicity (perhaps), present domicile, marital status, number and ages of children (if any), schools attended, occupation, job title, workplace, avocation and, maybe even political persuasion and religious affiliation.

Now, it should be obvious from the beginning that these self-descriptions are of the same nature as the descriptions given by onlookers. This is so, precisely because the former originates in the latter in the looking-glass experience. The self-description of Joycelyn could go on and on finally to rival the whole *Encyclopedia Britannica!* Yet, all the details can only add up to the statement, "This is *me*," and do not really answer the original query about her identity, her *I*. In other words, when she tried to clarify her *I*, she ended up talking endlessly about her *me*. Therein lies the irony. The unique person who is looking at herself to do all the sketching still lies hidden behind the collection of descriptors for social classification—"This is *me*"—which is in essence indistinguishable from anybody else's characterization of her—"This is she."

The reason for this strange turn of events is that the original, simple-sounding question is by nature not fully answerable. Like the out-of-scene puppeteer or masked Bunraku player, "The 'I' does not get into the limelight.... the 'I' is something that is never entirely calculable."[7] Hence, the only sensible answer to the question would have been the one Jehovah gave Moses a long time ago, namely, "I am who I am."[8]

Knowing the self by its picture. To recapitulate, "The 'I' is not a 'me' and cannot become a 'me'.... They are not identical."[9] The self is not fully representable in its picture, that is to say, in its image or concept. Just as there is much more to a person in the flesh than any portraits can show, the self has far more scope, complexity, and potential than our concept of that very self manages to capture. In that, *I* supersedes *me*. Save some transformative experiences illuminated by rare flashes of insight, the only possible way for us to honor the command of the Delphic oracle is to know one's self (*I*) via the tool of the self-concept (*me*). Therefore, it would be worth our while to study some additional features of this *notion* of who one is, or of the *picture* of what one is like.

As noted earlier, the initial self-concept is based upon a haphazard pile of social definitions, descriptions, and evaluations given by other people interacting with us. Another way of saying this is that we look in the surrounding mirrors and believe the images therein to be us, ourselves. That is why "it is impossible to conceive of a self arising outside of social experience."[10]

We have already mentioned, in relation to the formation of racial preferences, a very early onset of "the taking of the attitudes of others."[11] Since, in early years, these "others" are usually the family members, neighbors, and friends, the potential impact of their sustained, affect-laden interactions on the budding self is quite large. Through intimate contacts hourly and daily, they weave a tight fabric of human connectivity with which to wrap the young. Accordingly, the nature of experience within the child's microcosm is significant and, where positive, the internalized disposition can counteract the effects of negative attitudes held by others in the broader social contexts.

For example, studies of Morris Rosenberg and his associates showed that, contrary to their initial expectations, the self-esteem among urban black children and adolescents differed little from that of white youngsters.[12] Rosenberg later acknowledged that,

> My error lay in assuming that the prejudice that existed in the broader society was directly translated into the everyday life of the child.... [The fact is that] the opinions of "significant others" are more likely to have a powerful impact than the opinions of other people.... It is thus not the reflected appraisals of the broader society, most of which enter the child's experience in an indirect and muted form, but the views of those who interact with the children constantly and directly that have the most powerful effect on their self-esteem.[13]

The early drawing of the self-portrait. Many testimonies have been given to the lifelong significance of a positive view of oneself, acquired early with the help of those close to the person. From among the blacks, for instance, witnesses are easy to name, who have prevailed against the barriers of social prejudice and discrimination on the strength of their basic self-esteem nurtured within the family circle.[14] One of these remarkable people is Gordon Parks, a celebrated photographer, film director, painter, writer, poet, composer, and instrumentalist, who has given his tribute to his mother's early nurturing in the following words:

> I didn't know what lay ahead of me, but I believed in myself. My deepest instincts told me I would not perish. Poverty and bigotry would still be around, but at last I could fight them on even terms. The significant thing was a choice of weapons with which to fight them most effectively. That I would accept those of a mother who placed love, dignity and hard work over hatred was a fate that had accompanied me from her womb.[15]

Such fundamental self-trust certainly helps in navigating through the vicissitudes of life. Yet, thinking well of oneself does not, in itself, guarantee any constructive action. A case in point is seen in "the authoritarian personality," examined in a massive study of the psychological roots of anti-Semitism, undertaken shortly after the Second World War.[16] The researchers found that, among white, non-Jewish, native-born, middle-class Americans, the highly prejudiced ones held a very favorable opinion of themselves and also of their parents.

Meanwhile, they were not given to reflection or introspection, and did not tolerate ambivalent feelings in themselves. So, when things did not go their way, they typically blamed others instead of holding themselves responsible. In other words, conflicts within themselves were resolved by projecting their anxiety, and directing their hostility, outward onto members of the out-group (the Jew, the black, the Oriental, etc.). Stereotyping and scapegoating became the means for gaining "power over" others, while sustaining their self-glorification (and idealization of parents) in lieu of honest self-appraisal. Their effort was not "applied to achieving 'power of'—power of thought, power of understanding, power of growth.... a power that affirms life and [one's] own identity."[17]

Thus, the nurturing of that self- and life-affirming power of assessment and appreciation of oneself as a person may be characterized as one of the key accomplishments of the daily human interactions within the microcosm surrounding the young. "What we want [to see developing there] is justified self-confidence and self-esteem [since,] if we cannot have the originals, we can never have enough of the substitutes."[18] If the "power over" orientation becomes the substitute, one result could indeed be "narcissistic prejudices," involving "making use of the targets for the maintenance of self-esteem."[19] This would correspond to the third phase of extension transference in which people are seen as one's tools to be exploited as means to one's ends (see the last section of Chapter 3).

According to a study on children's views of foreign peoples, "the stereotyping process ...is not much in evidence with the 6-year-olds." Unfortunately, however, it "becomes very apparent in the early teen years.... Children apparently come to think about foreign peoples in an increasingly more stereotyped manner between 6 and 14 years."[20] Similarly, Gordon Allport observed that, by the age of seven or eight, many children get into the period of overgeneralization and total verbal rejection. This prejudicial tendency usually subsides a little later, but "by about age twelve ... verbal rejection is likely to have been replaced by the 'double talk' customary among adults who profess no prejudice while in fact demonstrating it. Verbal rejection (accompanied by behavioral acceptance) gives way to behavioral rejection (accompanied by verbal acceptance)."[21]

The fact that such changes become salient in early teen years is no coincidence, since

> in adolescence, self-esteem is a crucial problem. There is as yet little experience to base it on, and that little is a thoroughly biased sample acquired in the home and the juvenile group.... The adolescent building his appraisal of himself is therefore extremely vulnerable to the feelings and judgments expressed by the persons and institutions of his immediate environment. He is even more vulnerable than a child, because people mean more to him.[22]

Hopefully, "the universal adolescent needs of affection, esteem, security, recognition, and belonging are met" during this time. If not, however, "we find ourselves with adults who are frozen in time as children and constantly and loudly draw attention to themselves, or beg through their actions for acceptance and belonging."[23]

The tenacity of the picture-in-mind. One of the striking features of the self-concept or self-image is its tenaciousness in the face of new experiences, hence its stability over time. Once drawn, a person tends to believe in that particular picture of herself or himself as the whole truth, nothing but the truth about one's self. Like it or not, one gets used to that specific description of who one is. In the mind of the person,

$$\text{Self-concept} = \text{Self [or, } Me = I].$$

Once this equation is accepted, one might believe to know self well enough so as to become at ease with that self. However, as we saw above in the people of authoritarian personality, life built in correspondence with the picture-in-mind, even when it is flattering and likeable, does not necessarily prove wholesome in orientation. When the picture is less than favorable to begin with, any uncritical acceptance of that image as the truth can do much harm to one's self.

There is a 19th-century proverb that says, "Better the devil you know than the devil you don't know." It nicely captures the dynamics of the amazing stability of an established self-concept. For example, many children (mostly boys in this culture) experience considerable difficulties in learning to read, and they develop the idea of themselves as a bona fide non-reader. Some have even been known to dare their teachers to change them into a reader, if they [teachers] can—"Bet'cha you can't!" If the teacher were wise, he or she would not take up such a challenge as a simple matter of reading *skills* per se. Out of experience, the teacher would have learned that nobody can readily change a youngster who "knows" all about himself or herself. The pupil may not yet be able to read, but the child is quite convinced of who he or she is: "I *am* a non-reader [and proud of it!]" No ifs and buts about it—the little person would defend to death that picture of self, that familiar identity, that safe "truth." Indeed, "almost no one would give up who he or she is—one's own identity—to become someone else, even if the life were to be vastly better."[24] Who wants to become an unknown being, somebody one is *not*? Such a change is too daunting even to think about.

So, we should never underestimate the power of the known devil who dangles the luring, if false, sense of self-knowledge and security in the face of the terror of the unknown. How many of us have said, or at least wanted to say, to an acquaintance, "Just get out of such an abusive relationship, once and for all!" or "Shape up! Quit making the same mistake time and again!"? The advice was well meant, but not thoughtful enough to take into account the real difficulty of any drastic leap into a life as yet experienced. Unfortunately, there is a good reason why so many devastating liaisons, antisocial practices, and other destructive patterns of behavior persist and repeat themselves.

The hidden but powerful operation of the known devil is also seen in adolescents' efforts to arrive at their *own* identity. Many of them would forsake what they have grown up with and, in particular, renounce parental models. By so rejecting the *old*, they believe that they are creating the *new* for themselves. What they do not realize until much later, if at all, is that negation of the known devil cannot, in itself, lead to any positive definition of the unknown devil! This is because, as Paul Tillich pointed out, "The negative lives from the positive it negates."[25] Think of a photograph. The image appearing in the printed picture (the positive) is in fact compositionally identical with that on the film itself (the negative), isn't it? So, having said "No" to many of the beliefs, values, attitudes, and acts of our parents, we believed mistakenly that we had created a unique and [by definition] better identity for ourselves. What a shock it was, many years later, to discover how similar we actually were to our parents in how we tend to feel, reason, and act, and often even in our appearance, voice, and mannerism. Indeed, that old devil is a formidable one!

Distortions of images. A part of the devilishness of the looking-glass self is the inevitable distortions in the process of reflection. Mirrors do mirror, but a "mirror image" is not what this expression implies, namely, the sameness. The image is not the exact duplicate of the original face that is peering into the looking glass, and the inevitable distortion gets more and more pronounced as the image is reflected back and forth among many mirrors. As Dorothy Gilman describes it:

> One sees oneself never directly but through a line of mirrors that reflect back what neighbors, husbands, friends think and feel about us.... and by the time this reflection reaches us it's a graven image and not ourselves at all.[26]

Of course, young viewers do not even suspect that what they see may not really be who they are, and the nature and extent of such distortions tend to escape their attention for a long time. Here again, the *concept* of self as a cultural extension proves to be a double-edged sword. While the stability of the original picture of oneself, drawn early from the mirror reflections, can serve a constructive function, it may also hinder the person from reviewing and revising her or his self-image where and when needed for growth. Thus, a rude awakening may be experienced later in life, like the one that came to the 37-year-old woman we already met in Chapter 3.

> My whole focus was wrong.... The endlessness of reflecting myself in other people's eyes. Turn a pair of eyes on me and instantly I begin looking into them for myself. I seem to believe there is no Me except in other eyes. I am what I see in your eyes, whoever you are.[27]

Once again, we must remind ourselves of the power in the "tools" we have developed. In the instance of our *concept* of self, the same process of stereotyping, which is usually directed to other people, also applies to ourselves. In our mind, the particular stereotype comes to define who we are, either positively ("I *am* pretty, slow, dependable, dumb, etc.") or negatively ("I *am not* good at sports, mathematics, music, meeting people, etc."). We come to believe in it, and act accordingly, living up first to the social, and later to the self, expectations. This is the power of what Robert Merton called the self-fulfilling prophecy.[28] Like in all other cultural extensions, that power can benefit us when applied wisely. If used unawares or mindlessly, however, the same power will defeat us and hurt others.

The Two Pillars of the Self

Interestingly, the mirrors we hold up in social interactions tend to reflect back what each other *does* do much more clearly than who each other *is*. Especially in an action-oriented culture like ours, where deeds speak much louder than thoughts, and where all the feelings are to be worn outside on the sleeves, the merit of a person is judged primarily in terms of her or his *performance* (doing), not in reference to his or her *essence* (being). Ours is a culture wherein people have been noted to pursue "their own welfare…. with feverish ardor…. [by] the shortest path which may lead to it,"[29] and where the "inhabitants [are] all anxiously rushing about, always in a great hurry" even in their leisure.[30] Given this "impatience" and "strong drive for recognition,"[31] immediately visible deeds and short-term records of achievements become the central focus of attention.

Since adults clearly notice and react to it, children, while very young, find what they can *do* physically a major source of gratification as well as of frustration. Can a baby turn over, follow an object with eyes, sit up, crawl, stand, or walk? Is a child good at running, jumping with feet together, jumping rope, standing on head, pumping on a swing, keeping balance on an elevated bar, somersaulting, cartwheeling, skipping, whistling, two-wheel bicycling, or swimming? The list is practically endless, and can include talking, singing, reading, and writing. Granted all such acts of strength, sensory integration, and motor coordination are important early milestones, they can merely suggest a rough outline of the fast-changing, varied patterns of youngsters' development. What a child cannot do today for all her or his desire, determination, and efforts may pose little difficulty tomorrow. The only trouble is that children themselves find it difficult to believe this to be the case. They are disconsolate with their perceived inability to *do* these things, which they take to be permanent failures. They say, "I'll *never* be able to do that," and lose confidence in themselves. They are, in their mind, doomed forever.

To counteract the negative effects of this universal, disheartening experience, children must receive something more than consolation from adults for the temporary setbacks. What needs to be steadily built within each child is an appreciation of one's essential *being*, that is to say, a keen sense of the unique significance of oneself as a person. This awareness of one's fundamental worth should be relatively independent of what the individual can specifically do, and how well, at any given moment. That sense of basic specialness undergirds one's dignity. As Young put it, "Dignity is respect for what one is, feels and thinks…. It does not compare one with others for better or for worse because that is truly irrelevant. At heart, dignity is self-honesty and self-respect...."[32]

Where, in contrast, the *doing* aspect dominates in the judgment of one's self-worth (and the worth of others), the emphasis rests almost exclusively on action and performance, and the *being* dimension receives little attention. In such a milieu, not attaining, or losing, physical prowess spells a disaster. Thus, Robert Murphy who, at the height of his anthropology career, was felled by a tumor of the spinal cord, ascertained that, "Of all the psychological syndromes associated with disability, the most pervasive, and the most destructive, is a radical loss of self-esteem."[33] Understandably, dignity is hard to maintain or regain under such circumstances, as also attested by Arnold Beisser. He was an up-and-coming doctor in residency, and a former national collegiate tennis champion, when his life plans were abruptly truncated by polio. Remarkably, during three long years in an iron lung, he managed to gain the following insight and later went on to study and practice psychiatry as a paraplegic.

> I learned that to make a place for myself in the world, it was not always necessary to struggle, for I had a place already within me. As I became familiar with that place and increasingly trusting of it, I discovered that there was also a place for me in the world.[34]

The question then is how to nurture this all important *being* sense of self. Leading up to its consideration, let us first look at the ways in which the *doing* sense is cultivated.

Rewards and praises. Over the years, what Edward Thorndike noted in his 1898 dissertation, *Animal Intelligence*, has had a profound influence on the way we understand how any creatures, including *Homo sapiens*, learn. "[His] theory maintained that learning involves the wedding of a specific response to a specific stimulus through a physiological bond in the neural system, [and] the *bond* ... is 'stamped in' by being continually rewarded."[35] In other words, the particular response is more likely to recur when "it has previously been followed by 'a satisfying state of affairs.'"[36] In this associative interpretation, which was later fully adopted and elaborated upon by the school of behavioristic psychology, the "satisfying state of affairs" would be primarily provided from the outside. Thus, what is collectively defined as the correct and right performance is to be rewarded so as to increase the probability of its recurrence, which is seen as the sign of inward learning.

To give "positive reinforcement" to acts deemed desirable, especially of children, has become such a cliché in parenting and schooling that many people believe that showering lots of praises and rewards upon the learner, while avoiding anything remotely critical to say or show, is the universal key to success.[37] Marbles and M-&-M candies for doing some chores; smiling faces drawn on children's homework or artwork; gold stars posted next to pupils' names on the chalkboard;

laudatory scribbles on student assignments (such as "Excellent!" "A good job!" or "I agree with you"); the grade of *A* for courses taken at any level of schooling; cash bonuses or merchandise gifts for improved test scores, better grades, or higher job productivity—all such devices of praise and reward have thus come to be routinely applied for, allegedly, sustaining and enhancing the *doing* motivation and performance.

However, "the subtle danger in rewarding" has long been recognized by keen observers. A. S. Neill, among others, wrote that "rewards are superfluous and negative. To offer a prize for doing a deed is tantamount to declaring that the deed is not worth doing for its own sake."[38] The same opinion was voiced by Maria Montessori half a century earlier.

> If a child has to be rewarded or punished, it means he lacks the capacity to guide himself; so this has to be supplied by the teacher. But supposing he sets himself to work; then the addition of prizes and punishments is superfluous; they only offend the freedom of his spirit.[39]

His spirit gets offended precisely for the reason that,

> His dignity as a man is reduced to the limits of the dignity of a machine which must be oiled if it is to be kept going, because it does not have within itself the impulse of life.... All human victories, all human progress, stand upon the inner force.[40]

In more recent decades, alarms have been sounded over the wide-spread absence of "the impulse of life" in students whose primary goal for schooling has become "the acquisition of educational credentials—symbolic goods, such as grades, credits, and degrees—rather than the acquisition of useful skills and knowledge."[41] In other words, the collection of available external incentives has become a goal in itself, almost independently of the substance of learning: "As long as the tests are passed, credits are accumulated, and credentials are awarded, what occurs in most classrooms is allowed to pass for education,"[42] resulting in well schooled but poorly educated graduates.

Thus, as Jerome Bruner reminded his readers, "external reinforcement may indeed get a particular act going and may even lead to its repetition, but it does not nourish, reliably, the long course of learning ... what the world is and what it can be."[43] He could have added, "who one is and who one can be."

Regards and encouragement. So, even for the *doing* aspect of the sense of self, familiar incentives provided from the outside cannot really be depended upon to build the inner force needed for life-long development of a person. For the more basic, *being* sense of self, what is required is not judgmental reward and reinforcement, but mutual, steadfast trust and encouragement. The contrast between these two orientations is subtle but critical. First of all, the latter (trust and encouragement) is reciprocal, i.e., two way, in nature; while the former (praise, reward, and reinforcement) is essentially a unidirectional act. Second, the latter is focused upon the process, thus continuously operating irrespective of any particular result of a person's deed; meanwhile, the former is directly contingent upon the product, hinging upon the successful completion of an undertaking. Finally, the latter applies equally to the past, present, and future; while the former is strictly tied to past accomplishments.

It is certainly nice to receive compliments and prizes for something one has done, and done well. However, to build and sustain respect for, confidence in, and honesty with, one's self, everybody can use less accolades for one's deeds than a quiet acknowledgment of one's significance as a person, which is "the courtesy of the heart that respects the importance of another no matter"[44] who she or he is. This is especially true when one cannot *do* much, or is not *doing* fine, for one reason or another (e.g., young age, injury, infirmity, displacement, unemployment, emotional upheaval, task unfamiliarity or complexity) and, consequently, few rewards or reinforcements are forthcoming. Such would be exactly the circumstances under which the presence or absence of trust and encouragement spells a difference between persistence and renunciation.

Fortunately, the affirmation of the *essence* (being) of a person, apart from his or her *performance* (doing), does not require any elaborate maneuvers. Rather, it depends upon mutual recognition, that is to say, upon one's truly *seeing* the other as "a person wanted, respected, accepted as a human being worthy of dignity"[45] and, in turn, the other's knowing securely being so *seen*. According to Erik Erikson, "Those elements of numinosity, of seeing and being seen [are] basic for a sense of hope"[46]—a sense of hope for the humanity and of trust in one's self. Therefore, that seeing can be neither a cursory scanning nor a vacant staring. It must be a clear recognition and acknowledgment of the essence of each' s being, best captured in the word, "regard."

When we say, "Give my regards to your mother," for instance, the familiar expression conveys the double meanings of attentive looking and attendant respect. The courtesy of the heart to human dignity makes it essential that each interactant pay undivided attention to the other, thus seeing even as being seen, listening even as being listened to. Interestingly, it has been said that, in old Persia, the greatest tribute a king could pay any of his subjects was for just the two of them to saunter together in the beautiful, secluded royal garden. During that coveted stroll, the ruler was fully present to the ruled in spite of all the differences in the two stations of life. That human experience, more than the particular locale of its occurrence, is what the word, "paradise," was meant to convey.[47] And this same quality of unconditional regard and respect is what affirms a person's *being* and what nurtures the essence of his or her self.

Recapitualtion

Indications are that the initial, rough sketches, so to speak, of the person one perceives oneself to be are being executed fairly early on in life. For most people, these early portraits persist to influence later phases of their lives. Some striking testimonies to this may be culled from, among others, those who not only survived a wretched childhood but indeed prevailed over the circumstances to bloom into an admirable adulthood on the strength of the foundational image of who they are, can be, and should be.

For example, Gordon Parks recounts movingly: "My mother had freed me from the curse of inferiority long before she died by not allowing me to take refuge in the excuse that I had been born black. She had given me ambition and purpose, and set the course I had since traveled...."[49] It is obvious that "a child must be loved, given authoritative [*not* authoritarian] views of appropriate behavior, and motivated to put forth the effort to do the best he or she can. Competence [derives primarily] from the combination of firm guidance and loving support that the child receives."[50]

Nonetheless, even with a less than favorable start, "people *can* change their lives...,"[51] by utilizing the same extension at hand, namely, the self-portrait itself. Indeed, given the basically interactive process of its drawing,[52] elaborations and modifications of the image or concept of self are inevitable under any circumstances. As the child's world expands beyond the microcosm of the family and then the neighborhood, divergent settings for his or her thoughts, feelings, and acts will continue to multiply in number and increase in complexity. Differing, and often conflicting, social expectations are likely to lead to many context-specific "selves" with varying degrees of overall coherence, i.e., coordination and integration.

Many revisions will be made, willy-nilly, to the earlier portraits, even if the overall composition, tone, and the like tend to remain the same. In some instances, nevertheless, a radical reworking on the original may be, or may have to be, made to initiate, or better represent, the changes in the person herself or himself. After all, "early competence does not guarantee mature competence; it merely makes it more likely.... [Meanwhile,] individual determination can bring about change throughout the life course."[53]

Let us now examine the nature of the life course itself.

Notes

1. Douglas and Ney, 1998.
2. Cooley, 1902, 183.
3. Winnicott, 1988, 61.
4. Sullivan, 1953.
5. G. Mead, 1964, 204.
6. Goodman, 1964, 252, 253.
7. G. Mead, 1964, 229, 233. For an erudite analysis, see Ricoeur, 1992.
8. Exod. 3:14.
9. G. Mead, 1964, 229, 233
10. Ibid., 204.
11. Ibid., 229.
12. Rosenberg, 1965; Rosenberg and Simmons, 1972.
13. Rosenberg, 1989, xx.
14. E.g., Comer, 1988; Gates, 1994; Mathabane, 1987; McBride, 1997; Thornton, 1996.
15. Parks, 1986, 274.
16. Adorno, Frenkel-Brunswick et al., 1950. Similar observations have been offered in more recent sources such as Bushman and Baumeister, 1998; Emler, 2001; and Seligman, 1998. The complex dynamics of "high vs. low" self-esteem was discussed in, e.g., Baumeister, 1993.
17. Montagu, 1998, 240.
18. Hoffer, 1964, 4.
19. Young-Bruehl, 1996, 233.
20. Lambert and Klineberg, 1967, 211-212.
21. Allport, 1961, 309. Also see, Allport, 1958.
22. Friedenberg, 1962, 107.
23. Wigginton, 1986, 234-235.
24. Brim, 1992, 83.
25. Tillich, 1952, 176.
26. Gilman, 1989, 23-24.
27. Koller, 1983, 94.
28. Merton, 1949.
29. Tocqueville, 1991, 144.
30. Barzini, 1984, 238.
31. Hall and Hall, 1989, 149.
32. Young, 1966, 129.
33. Murphy, 1990, 90.
34. Beisser, 1990b, 170. Also see, Kurland, 2002.
35. Cremin, 1964, 111.

36. Bruner, 1966, 127-128.
37. It should be recalled that the original definition of the *positive* reinforcement was in terms of any stimuli that *increase* the probability of recurrence of a given response. It has little to do with the particular variety of the stimulus, so long as it boosts, for whatever reasons, the likelihood of repeated performance. Even though they are typically believed to be *positive* reinforcements, *comforting* words, *kind* deeds, or *desirable* commodities may or may not elicit such effects. Indeed, under any particular circumstances, they may even turn out to be *negative* reinforcements and serve to *decrease* the probability of the expected recurrence of a given response.
38. Neill, 1960, 162.
39. Montessori, 1969, 245.
40. Montessori, 1964, 22, 24.
41. Labaree, 1997, 251. Also see, Drucker, 1969; Sachs, 1996; Steinberg, 1996.
42. Sedlak et al., 1986, 183. The usurpation of the inherent interest in substantive learning by the accumulation of external incentives (i.e., such extensions as certain letter grades, choice class tracks, and parental bribes) is an instance of what Allport, 1937, identified as the phenomenon of "functional autonomy."
43. Bruner, 1966, 128. Also see, Kohn, 1993.
44. Young, 1966, 127-128.
45. Axline, 1964, 216.
46. Erikson, 1977, 144.
47. E.g., Laye, 1975.
48. Also see, Yamamoto, 1988. The phrase, "the unconditional acceptance," was made popular by, notably, Rogers, 1961.
49. Parks, 1986, 273-274.
50. Clausen, 1995, 526.
51. Ibid., 521.
52. In passing, it should be noted that, in the European tradition, the "interactive" nature of this portrait drawing (i.e., the self-image formation) is understood mostly in terms of the interactions between the self and the other (people). Elsewhere, however, the process may more integrally encompass the interactions between the self and the physical environment (objects and nature in general). See, e.g., Berque, 1993, 1994; Lifton, 1968, 1976; and Rosenberger, 1994, on the Japanese sense of self. On the other hand, we may have been blithely ignoring the far more diverse perspectives in the Western past itself so as to conform to the current, unitary notion. See, e.g., Murray, 1993; also, Myrdal, 1969.
53. Clausen, 1995, 522.

Chapter 5. Stories of Life

There is a Japanese adage that says, "The spirit of a child of three holds true even at one hundred." Although it nicely highlights the lasting and pervasive power of the extension named the self-concept or self-image, it errs in suggesting an immutability of one's sense of personal identity over a long period of time. While all the sketches and portraits of oneself are of the given moments, life has to be lived continuously across seasons and to be made sense of accordingly. Thus, yet another form of cultural extension is called into play, and that is the *story* of the ever-changing life. As Henri Bergson put it,

> the moments of time and the positions of the mobile are only snapshots which our understanding has taken of the continuity of movement and duration. In these juxtaposed views one has a practical substitute for time and movement... but time and movement are something else.... [T]he essence of duration is to flow, and ... the fixed placed side by side with the fixed will never constitute anything which has duration. It is not the "states," simple snapshots we have taken ... along the course of change, that are real; on the contrary... it is change itself that is real.[1]

So, instead of, or in addition to, a collection of snapshots we keep for ourselves and show to each other, we create something like a movie that tells a story of the *course* of our life. Indeed, 'we cannot help thinking in terms of stories... [since] it is the *only* way we can make sense of the world.'[2]

The Storyteller

The ordinary daily operation of the human mind has thus been likened to the art of narrative, of creating and telling of stories. "Anyone at any age is able to tell the story of his or her life with authority. Everyone all the time is in the act of composition.... and people find the meaning of their lives in the idea of sequence, in conflict, in metaphor and in moral."[3]

So, we expand over time from still pictures of ourselves to a movie, from the photography to the cinematography. Regardless of the quality of the individual snapshots, they now are to be arranged with proper commentaries so as to form as coherent a narrative as possible. The result is the *story* of one's life, understandable to oneself and worth telling to others. This extension, derivative of the primary one of the self-portrait, is familiar to all, but some of its interesting features may escape our attention.

To begin with, every person makes up his or her own story. Although the given "culture and society to which we adhere gives us the framework of that story,"[4] the actual construction of the particular script is ultimately an individual matter. So, each person is the unmistakable *author* of the account of life. However, this story is not merely for telling—it has also to be lived. Therefore, the author must simultaneously be the *actor*, the protagonist in the script. That actor, meanwhile, had better be advised and coached by somebody on how best to perform the stipulated role. Cultural mores again provide certain broad guidelines but, in the end, the person herself or himself must be the *director* of the drama. Finally, the same author-actor-director also serves as the most intimate *audience/critic* of the whole rendition.[5]

This inescapable, concurrent assumption of multiple functions is undoubtedly demanding, and may contribute to the common difficulties at crucial transitional points, for instance, during adolescence and in the so-called mid-life crisis. However, it also provides us with certain opportunities for a unique and variable writing, directing, acting, and critiquing all along our course of life. As Aldous Huxley said, "Experience is not what happens to you, it's what you do with what happens to you."[6] In fact, we can rewrite our stories at any point, and thus change both the what and the how of our living significantly. Unlike in literary pieces, it is not imperative that our storyline be seamless in consistency. We are *not* destined to live the story as if it were immutable. How it has been developed in the earlier chapters does not necessarily bind us in beginning a new chapter to stay true to that particular script. This allows us, as the author, actor, director, and audience/critic, quite a bit of freedom in applying initiative, ingenuity, and flexibility in changing our story and performance—that is to say, our life itself. A dramatic conversion of Simon from a simple fisherman to a man that caught men as St. Peter, or that of Saul from a rabid anti-Christian to a pillar, as St. Paul, of Christendom, is a classic case in point.

Much less striking yet no less palpable examples of the life-changing capacity of the creation of revised stories have been variously labeled as the instances of the "self-fulfilling prophecy," "Pygmalion effects," "power of positive thinking," "positive illusions," and so on.[7] Where the change runs in the negative direction, meanwhile, a more descriptive name may be the "Frankenstein effects"![8] The dynamics is the same: what a person creates and believes in, whether depicted in her or his concept of self or told in his or her story of life, makes a difference in that person's life. It is in this formative, as well as transformative, sense that we may read Tillich's statement: "Man creates what he is.... Man is what he makes of himself. And the courage to be as oneself is the courage to make of oneself what one wants to be.... Courage is self-affirmation 'in spite of'...."[9]

To Remember

Thus, the life narrative can serve as the catalytic device with which to shift the course of one's life *in spite of* many constrictions, past and present, external and internal. However, as with any other cultural extensions we routinely use, most of us remain unaware of our dependence on the device and of its power, constructive as well as destructive. "We are all story-telling animals.... We prefer to think that we speak only what is true.... But...we seem to forget that all stories are subjective truths, and then [we believe] we are compelled to live our lives as though they were the stories told."[10] In this extension transference, we equate the *story* of life with *life* itself. As the stories remain unchanged, so shall the lives be.

Now, the irony is that any reworking, if at all, of the narrative appears much easier and more prevalent in the direction of the past than in the present and towards the future. That is to say, most of us do change, intentionally or unintentionally, our stories *retroactively*. "Because I am thinking about the past these days," observed May Sarton, I have come to see that the past is always changing, is never static, never 'placed' forever like a book on a shelf. As we grow and change, we understand things and the people who have influenced us in new ways."[11] In other words, our memories are not like the Rosetta stone, guarding the carved hieroglyphic secret for years to come.

But why change the message at all? Gilbert Brim believes as follows:

> That we change our memories to increase our self-respect is widely understood. Less well understood is how we alter our memories to create coherent stories of our lives that explain our place in life and account for what happened to us.... [T]he past must be revised to fit the present and the future, creating the appearance of an orderly process of development from beginning to end.... In this sense, the present and the future determine the past.[12]

In the common, narrative memory, therefore, the mind organizes various experiences into a reasonably consistent story of life that is consonant with the image of self and thus serves to sustain a sense of continuity of one's identity across time and space. "Memory ... enables people to maintain the illusion of continuity. Because of memory, lives *appear* to have continuity. "[13] We create consonant experience by making some changes to "what happened to us" (to borrow Huxley's earlier quoted expression), and then remember the results in memory. "If the adjustment helps to make the overall value system more coherent and functional, memory distortion may very well serve a benign purpose."[14]

Indeed, "Successful adaptation takes place when individuals symbolically connect meaningful past experiences with current circumstances.... [C]onstruction and interpretation of experience as one grows older are found to be critical elements that give form and meaning to one's actions."[15] While the particular choices our mind makes are still largely a mystery as to *what* it remembers or forgets *when* and *why*, it is increasingly clear that one's past must stay alive in the present if it were to help shape a better future, since "it is precisely this process of reconciling the past today in order to live better tomorrow that remains the essence of living with the tensions and challenges of a lifetime."[16]

However, this integrative function is disrupted if some parts of one's past are set aside to make them not readily available for the narrative construction. They then come to belong in the so-called implicit memory, which is there in the person to continue to affect her or his life without, unlike the explicit memory, remaining associated with the original experiential context and being available to conscious scrutiny and regulation. These particular experiences are banished from one's awareness due, for instance, to some overwhelming sentiments of humiliation, shame, anguish, guilt, and the like. Whatever the precise reason might be, the results are a split within oneself. Certain existential components are detached and isolated from the rest and, hence, cannot be worked into the overarching story. Accordingly, such "disrupted, disjunctive memory" makes the resultant narrative an especially incomplete representation of the self, namely, the whole person.[17] Any such experiences "preclude communication [but, ironically] they require communication ... because without expression the sense of ... shame cannot be expiated, and reality cannot be confirmed.... In telling about it, we restructure or re-contextualize the experience, we make sense of it.... The experience is better 'integrated' when we tell it, because the telling 'proves' that it is real."[18]

On the other hand, the *telling* of an experience can itself follow a less than constructive bent, and the *sense-making* may be accomplished by creating a more or less fictional memory. After all, as we have been noticing, "memory is not a fixed thing.... It is a process [and], in the formation of a memory, current beliefs about past events are more important than what actually happened."[19] Moreover, "our brains are built to remember the gist of things, not the details.... As we spin our tale, calling on the large items for the schema of our past memory, we simply drag into the account likely details that could have been part of the experience.... This sort of memory invention is false memory at work."[20] In extreme instances, nothing needs to have happened to the storyteller, and the gist of the story may originate in other stories he or she has heard being told. A case in point is the astonishing one of Bruno Grosjean, also known as Binjamin Wilkomirski, a self-proclaimed Latvian Jew, who wrote a powerful, detailed memoir of a harrowing Holocaust childhood, which became a literary sensation much touted by discriminating writers and critics—for a while, anyway. However, a later investigation by a Swiss journalist cast serious doubts about his claimed identity and the authenticity of the recounted experience. After a painstaking investigation of his own, another reporter came to the conclusion that Grosjean actually grew up in the neutral Switzerland throughout the Second World War years and wrote the book wholly by reclaiming "the memories of others" as his own. "That's what Wilkomirski has done, decking himself out in second-hand memories, borrowed memories, and outright stolen memories."[21]

This was indeed an exceptional case, but it is generally known that the particular socio-historical milieu and the suggestions of those significant in people's lives strongly bias their perceptions of the past experiences.[22] Accordingly, "Memory is not simply a personal, subjective experience. It is socially constructed and present oriented and thus reconfigured experience."[23] In recent years, alarm has been sounded over the "'pseudomemories' that are induced by some therapists and hypnotists."[24] Of course, "it is clear that suggestion independent of hypnosis may exert a powerful influence on memory retrieval,"[25] but such people of professional authority, in particular, can even inadvertently "implant ... the idea that some untoward event happened... in earlier years."[26] All sorts of abuses and molestations in childhood and thereafter, the brain washing by satanic cults or some popular social movements, and even abductions by space aliens may be, and have in fact been, claimed by many. Interestingly, hypnosis seems to add to the confidence of the clients in the stories they are to tell rather than to the accuracy of the memory as such.[27] Therefore, these pseudomemories tend to be quite self-convincing, even as the stories are likely to become increasingly more elaborate.[28]

Typically accompanying such memory disruption and disjunction is the tendency that a singular, traumatizing event in the reconstituted past comes to define all of the present and future, leaving the person forever a victim, blaming somebody else in his or her survivor narrative.[29] For that reason, the Swiss journalist Daniel Ganzfried, who had first unmasked the charade of Bruno Grosjean, summarized the three most offensive elements "about Wilkomirski's book and his persona as a survivor" as follows:

> 1. The child victim, remaining both, child and victim, for the rest of his life. 2. The never ending Holocaust, once in Auschwitz, you stay in there, forever, no matter what you do and what happens to you, which of course means the victim as sick person for the rest of his life, prey for analysts and therapists. 3. The pornography of violence in re: the Holocaust.[30]

Continuity and consistency in life may thus be purchased at a very high price.

To Be Remembered

Granted that the Grosjean variety of false memories are far more spectacular, and hopefully rarer, than most, and granted also that the human brains are said to provide a ready mechanism for false narratives,[31] what would be the motives for such fabrications after all? In the first instance, there appears to be no need to implicate any sinister plots or diabolical schemes on the part of common individuals. The basic dynamics was nicely illustrated by Susan Allen Toth in her experiences following the publication of her autobiograhical novel. Numerous letters from her readers and the direct interactions with some of them on book-signing occasions impressed her with "the hunger of 'ordinary' people to have their lives recorded and valued.... Readers said again and again ... 'You've told my story'.... The importance of being remembered ... came home poignantly...."[32]

No one likes to be a nobody. Everyone wants to be remembered, at least by someone, anyone, to be somebody. That yearning translates itself into, among others, career endeavors to be listed in the *Who's Who*, serious or whimsical exploits recorded in *Guiness Book of Records*, generous deeds of charity and devotion, heroic acts of courage and valor, genealogical interests in one's roots, and happy or sad family reunions. It also leads some to destructive acts for notoriety. "The universal demand for attention, approval, and acceptance, the insistent 'watch me' of children (and adults?) is the delineation of oneself as a leading character in the narrative of life."[33]

However, there can be some deeper significance in the prevalent desire to be remembered, since such a yearning may be reflective of the endless human quest for immortality. John Cowper Powys argued that, "In only one way can our mortal and, it may be, our immortal life be bravely, thoroughly, and absolutely justified, and that way is by *treating it as a story*."[34] Malcom Cowley likewise recommends for people, particularly those of advanced ages, to look back over their respective lives to see a certain, identifiable pattern in them. "Our lives that seemed a random and monotonous series of incidents are something more than that: each of them has a plot."[35] That sort of reflection, self-initiated or other-catalyzed (like some of Toth's readers), tends to change one's perceptions of what her or his life may have been about.

For instance, on her 72nd birthday, Truitt wondered: "May we not each of us evolve so entirely within a larger teleology that our lives are woven, warp and woof and willy-nilly," into an immense weft, "every human being adding some essential singularity to the pattern of humankind?"[36] The same thought was expressed in a different analogy by Eiseley when he wrote that "an order of life is like a diamond of many reflecting surfaces, each with its own pinpoint of light contributing to the total effect."[37] In such transcendental perspective one senses immortality. "What is important for memory and story is that a man's deeds be worth remembering, worth telling…," says John Dunne. "The things of his life, if we list them, are the same as they were before, but … his relationship [to them can become] different. He may have a story now that is worth telling…. His deeds begin to seem worthy of being remembered, worthy of living on in memory, worthy of becoming immortal in story."[38]

In psychological terms, "The 'I' coordinates what has been called a 'narrative configuration,' through which we 'make our existence into a whole by understanding it as an expression of a single unfolding and developing story.'"[39] The sense of immortality hinges upon this sense-making of one's life across space, over time —a forming of "a symbolic relationship toward that which has gone on before, and that which we know will go on after, what we realize to be our own finite individual lives."[40] All told, the narratives are a powerful extension indeed at our disposal for structuring, orienting, and restructuring life.

Living and storytelling. "A life is not 'how it was,'" says Jerome Bruner, "but how it is interpreted and reinterpreted, told and retold…. [Thus,] we *become* the autobiographical narratives by which we 'tell about' our lives."[41] Does this then mean that "we *are* the stories we tell"? No, it is still necessary to keep in mind that this expression is another example of extension transference that can easily lead us astray. Just as "the symbol is NOT the thing symbolized; the word is NOT the thing; the map is NOT the territory it stands for,"[42] the self-concept is NOT the self, and the story of life is NOT the life itself.

> It seems entirely obvious that in life we deal with an enormous number of things and situations, "feelings", which are *not verbal*. These belong to the "objective level". The crucial difficulty is found in the fact that whatever can be said *is not* and *cannot* be on the objective level, but belongs *only* to the verbal level. This difference, being *inexpressible* by words, cannot be expressed by words.[43]

When the more abstract notions, images, or stories are blithely mistaken for the more direct, complex, and "unspeakable" experiences of life itself, we start living an imitation of life. Hans Christian Anderson's emperor triumphantly marched up the main street, with all suitable pomp and circumstance, into his impressive palace and elegant throne. Actually stark naked, yet quite confident of the resplendence of his noble, invisible attire, he was in fact living a lie among his stunned subjects, wasn't he?

Of course, the mistake the hapless emperor was making is a very common one. Unawares, he believed in the fiction of an original, magnificent vestment, carefully constructed and sustained by his disloyal ministers and greedy merchants, so as to ignore the need to ascertain its veracity against the real state of his dressiness. Thus, he had believed in the pleasant narrative of a life, and mistaken the *story* so told for his own *life*—until that innocent child revealed the grievous error in the emperor's judgment.

Notes

1. Bergson, 1975, 16.
2. Smith, 1990, 64.
3. Doctorow, 1985.
4. Smith, 1990, 65.
5. Cowley, 1982.
6. Huxley, 1932, Introduction.
7. These phrases are from, respectively, Merton, 1949; Rosenthal and Jacobson, 1989; Peale, 1952; and Taylor, 1989.
8. Gaylin, 1991; Yamamoto, 1993.
9. Tillich, 1952, 150-151.
10. Beisser, 1990a, 41.
11. Sarton, 1981, 95.
12. Brim, 1992, 85.
13. G. Becker, 1999, 180.
14. Kammen, 1997, 330.
15. Kaufman, 1986, 162-163.
16. Erikson, Erikson, and Kivnick, 1986, 104.
17. Langer, 1991.
18. Cottle, 1980, 254.
19. Tavris, 1993, 16.
20. Gazzaniga, 1998, 142-143.
21. Gourevitch, 1999, 68.
22. Baker, 1996.
23. G. Becker, 1999, 180.
24. Tavris, 1993, 17.
25. Spiegel, 1997, 138.
26. Gazzaniga, 1998, 146.
27. Spiegel, 1997.
28. Gazzaniga, 1998.
29. Rieff, 1991.
30. Gourevitch, 1999, 65. Many book reviewers were totally duped by Bruno Grosjean's charade. However, the mental damage his memory theft inflicted upon some of the relatives of the Holocaust victims or upon the few child survivors themselves has been much more profound. See, e.g., Eskin, 2002.
31. Gazzaniga, 1998.
32. Toth, 1987, 37.
33. Smith, 1990, 66.
34. John Cowper Powys, quoted in Cowley, 1982, 71.
35. Cowley, 1982, 71.
36. Truitt, 1984, 179.

37. Eiseley, 1980, 85.
38. Dunne, 1975, 22, 23.
39. Lifton, 1993, 91.
40. Lifton, 1987, 13. 39.
41. Bruner, 1987, 31, 15.
42. Hayakawa, 1964, 30.
43. Korzybski, 1948, 416.

Chapter 6. Devices of the Storyteller

Storytelling is an art form. In life, just as in literature and theater, good storytellers muster all the skills of the trade to enrich their creation and enhance their performance. An impressive store of cultural extensions is available for that purpose, even though most of us have not mastered what they are and how to use them. Some among the paraphernalia deserve particular attention because of their fundamental nature and the extensiveness of their application. Two of them are called abstraction and analogy.

Abstraction

Abstraction is a convenient way of *making sense* of the world within and without. The process allows us to read some sort of order into the baffling multitude of objects, creatures, phenomena, experiences, and everything else in life by the double operations of grouping and labeling. It is another, powerful, continuously employed extension at our disposal.

The concrete. At very concrete levels—that is to say, before abstractions really begin—our encounters with the world including ourselves are immediate and actually indescribable. If one came across, in the dark of the forest or in the depth of the ocean, some strange creature never seen before, one would be hard pressed to believe, to begin with, in the very reality of that sighting. Even when finally convinced of the existence of this *thing*, and even with the facilities for drawing or talking, it would be difficult to come up with precise descriptions, much less any proper understanding, of the nameless monster.

More to the point, in the presence of the sacred and the supreme that surpass our level of comprehension, we stand in awed silence. Likewise, in the face of the wretched and the tragic that defy human sensibility, word again fails us. The concrete encounter is powerful enough to leave us speechless, and the experience remains unspeakable, inexpressible. For example, when Moses came across the mysterious burning bush on Mount Sinai and received God's command to lead the Israelites out of Egypt, he hesitated and asked the name of the Holiest. The answer given, though verbal, reveals the nature of such direct meeting: "I am who I am." God *is* —no abstraction should be necessary here. One should know the presence of the Almighty through direct experience, not by any other names, not through any idols, and not in any graven images. All such representations are abstractions at one level or another.

To abstract. Of the grouping and naming operations of abstraction, the learning begins early in everyday life. Think, for example, of young children's emotional experiences. Initially, all they have is what they vaguely sense in their bodies to which they react physiologically and behaviorally. Watchful adults may observe a stiffening of the whole body or some parts thereof; an assumption of certain postures or gestures; changes in skin color, facial expression, or breathing; disturbance of elimination, sleeping, and other bodily functions; and, of course, crying. From such indications, grown-ups surmise what must be happening in the children and respond with, hopefully, an appropriate action of comfort, assurance, affirmation, and so on. Equally significant for children's development, however, is the accompanying adult verbalizations that show the young how to choose *proper* labels to attach to the global, theretofore unidentified, kinesthetic sensations. Through such expressions as "Don't be *afraid*, Honey, Mommy is right here!" "Oh boy, you are real *angry*, aren't you?" "What's the matter? You look *sad* this morning?" "Is it a sharp *pain* around here?" or "You like this a lot, don't you, my *happy* one?!" the message is sent for the suitable differentiation and naming of the various feelings.

In time, the initially *unsorted, unnamed* organismic reactions come to be identified by the consensual words, i.e., labels, like fear, anger, sadness, pain, and happiness. "A person in any state of high emotion demonstrates 'generalized physiological arousal'.... Differences among the emotions stem from the labels we happen to assign to the state of arousal.... What we call emotions are essentially *cultural performances*, learned and enacted on appropriate occasions."[1] Proper names and "performances" make the interpersonal communication and understanding much easier. That is what abstracting allows us to do and, early on, children add this powerful cultural extension to their paraphernalia.

Labeling. However, the names themselves do not necessarily clarify the nature of what or who have been so named or the interrelationships among what have been clustered into differing groups. How many, totally dissimilar Bobs, Bills, Helens, or Sues does each of us know? Or, think of Judaism, Christianity, and Islam. These labels do not convey any sense of the basic commonality among the three major religions of the world, namely, their monotheism. Indeed, the dissimilarity of the labels tends to suggest some fundamental differences among them rather than any parallels or overlaps. Naming is just for convenience, and most labels have not been systematically selected on the basis of some formal, underlying schemes like the classic, genus-species taxonomy of Linnaeus for living things.

Thus, the Tower of Babel continues to stymie us. "Stern," "星" (pronounced, ho-shi, in Japanese), "stella," "ἄστρο," and "star" are different codes for the same thing, but many of us would not know it. We can also wonder, jokingly, why it is that *every single* rooster in France mysteriously (!) makes time by always crowing "Co-co-ri-co!," one in Italy Chicchi-ri-chi!," that in the United Kingdom "Cock-a-doodle-doo!," one in Spain "Qui-qui-ri-qui!," that in Japan "Kokke-kokko!," and one in Germany "Ki-ke-ri-ki!" Meanwhile, even in the same code (language), different names may be given to the same objects. To give just a few examples, those who use Queen's English put their suitcases in the "boot" of their cars, not in the "trunk," and pay for their purchases at the store's "tills," not at the "cash registers." In the U.S., students may study music at a "conservatory," which is unlikely to be the kind of a sunroom attached to some British houses. Finally, woe to any Americans walking around in public, only donning "pants" without a proper pair of "trousers" to cover the underwear!

It seems so obvious that "the *word*, the *label* ... is *not* the thing,"[2] but the confounding of labels with things is quite prevalent and persistent.

Generalization

Added to this easy confusion between the names and the named is the oft-confounding power of generalization. Together, labeling and generalization make abstraction a truly potent device for our thinking and story telling, and also an omnipresent source of trapping. That is to say, once things are placed in the same clusters and labeled the same, we forget all about any other differences among the individual elements and handle them as identical. The basic classification itself is seldom a straightforward affair, since most objects, people, or phenomena do not naturally cluster into neat, separate groups (i.e., categories). So, the application of given criteria must typically be done on a discretionary basis, ignoring other particulars and contexts. Anybody who ever got totally frustrated by the Yellow Pages (phone directories), trying to find the *right* category for the desired goods or services can appreciate the difficulties involved in setting up any uniformly acceptable classification scheme.

Nevertheless, once the abstraction process begins on whatever basis, all the elements in the same cluster are called by the same categorical name and treated identically while being regarded to be clearly different from the elements in any other clusters. The twin assumptions of (1) the sameness within a given category, and (2) the distinctiveness from all other categories, are shown in all classification attempts. What this allows us to do is to *equalize within* and *differentiate without*. Thus, what applies to one element or member is by definition applicable to all other elements or members in that particular category, but it is inapplicable to any elements or members of differently labeled categories. So, in Figure 6-1, each of the clusters like "Great Dane," "Saint Bernard," "Shepherd," "Hound," "Terrier," "Poodle," or "Chihuahua" would include all individual creatures so named, regardless of the myriad variations within the group in age, size, shape, weight, color, vitality, intelligence, temperament, and so on. Purebred terriers are terriers no matter how different they may actually be from each other while, by definition, none of them is a hound. However, terriers and hounds, together with numerous other groups can be subsumed under a larger category called "Dog" at one level up the "abstraction ladder."[3]

On the same rung of this ladder where "Dog" is located, that is to say, at the same level of abstraction, such other clusters as "Cat" and "Bear," "Ape" and "Man," "Whale" and "Dolphin" are to be found, and these, in turn, may be grouped into, respectively, "Carnivore," "Primate," and "Cetacean." At the next higher level of abstraction, these three can be clustered with other categories into "Mammal," and so on and so forth.

Now, notice a couple of interesting features of this "ladder." First of all, the number of different ladders that can be built is quite large, even starting from exactly the same elements, since any aspect of those elements may be chosen for abstracting purposes. For instance, dogs do not have to be categorized by breed or morphology (form and structure). They can be grouped by use (sheep dog, hunting

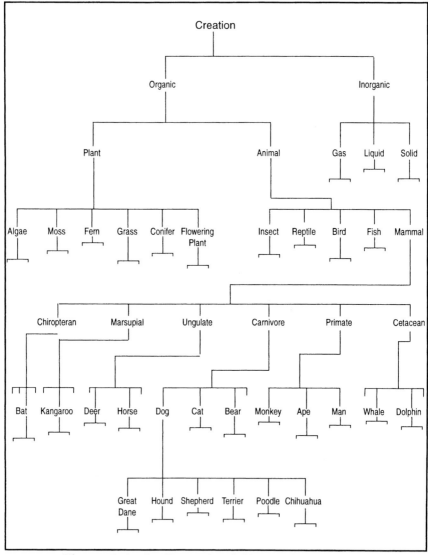

Figure 6-1. An Example of Abstraction Ladders

dog, rescue dog, guard dog, racing dog, guide dog, companion dog, etc.), color, size, fur type, locale of origin, and so forth, and, furthermore, any dog may be cross-classified in two or more such categories (e.g., seeing-eye dogs with long hair). Also, there is no fixed number of the rungs, that is to say, of the levels of abstraction, either. For instance, before moving up to the "Mammal" level in Figure 6-1, another layer of abstraction may be easily laid by grouping the "Primate" level categories simply into two clusters, "Aquarian" and "Terrestrial."

The point is that how a specific ladder is built depends upon what it is for, and there is no "one and only" way to construct it. Any particular classification system is adopted by someone for convenience and sustained mostly by tacit agreement of others. Think of the aisles and shelves of supermarkets. Even within a single chain, *which* specific merchandise is to be found *where* tends to vary from store to store, and sometimes from week to week within the same store (!), so as to cause endless aggravation of the customers. In fact, no grouping decision can escape some measure of arbitrariness, but familiarity with the particular arrangements reduces confusion. Thus, it is only the hapless tourists who must find out by the hard way the contrast between the "Apotheke" and the "Drogerie" in Germany, between the "Boucherie" and the "Charcuterie" in France, or between the "Taxi" and "Minicab" in England.[4] "Classification," says Hayakawa, "is not a matter of identifying 'essence,' as is widely believed. It is simply a reflection of social convenience and necessity—and different necessities are always producing different classifications."[5]

Why abstract? So, to sum up, what special power of extension does abstraction give us? The answer lies in the fact that abstracting is the basic process through which humans order their experiences and make sense of them. This function can be seen clearly in young children each of whom must construct some scheme of comprehension in the face of initially chaotic encounters with all sorts of things, creatures, and events. In the absence of such a scheme, sometimes also called a cognitive map, what-belongs-where and what-relates-to-what will be unclear, and the whole experience remains a baffling chaos. Without order, life is formless, incomprehensible, and devoid of meaning.

Thus, as the title of one of Jean Piaget's books reads, "to understand is to invent,"[6] that is, to create an organizing scheme for sense-making. The so-called reality does not sit *out there*, ready-made for all. Rather, it must be tailor-made by each person to be constructed *internally* through (a) identifying what is similar, as well as disparate, among the multitudes of individual things, creatures, events, and experiences, (b) grouping these elements into small clusters, (c) labeling each cluster, (d) identifying the similarities and differences among these clusters themselves, (e) grouping the clusters into a smaller number of larger clusters, (f) labeling the larger clusters, (g) repeating the process until an overall classification scheme has been built with increasingly more subsumptive categories. Without such foundational work of abstraction, no coherent view of the world is possible, no clear concept of self could be formed, no intelligible story of life would be told, and no sustainable human relations may be woven.

The construction of one's reality is a task required of each person. Nevertheless, children do not have to start from nothing, since (i) the range and variety of the elements amenable to abstraction are reasonably uniform in a given ecological setting and specific historical epoch; (ii) the prototypical schemes of comprehension are a part of their cultural legacy, just as the available extensions; and (iii) the modeling and guidance functions, whether inter- or intra-generational, are integral to any group life. As a result, certain ease of communication and understanding is to be expected within a communal group.

Now, the generalization involved in any abstracting operations also enables us to "bind time" so that "each generation of humans, at least potentially, can start where the former generation left off."[7] Because higher-level abstractions like ideas, principles, and theories are much more generalizable than lower-level ones, they can be examined, discussed, recreated, or revised even after the concrete events and acts are long gone. "[Higher-level abstractions] may be preserved and used over and over again in extra-neural forms, as recorded in books and otherwise.... and they can be put back in the nervous system as *active neural processes.* The above represents a fundamental mechanism of time-binding which becomes overwhelmingly important."[8] Thus, especially with the help of some other extensions like words and codes, pictures, models, or even buildings, they can be studied and utilized across generations, thus making fleeting time less relevant. Of course, it may be said that higher-level abstractions bind space too, since the generalized concepts like wine, black hole, cancer, ethics, or beauty can be explored not only any*time* but also any*where*, terrestrial or extraterrestrial, thereby making the concrete spatial contexts comparatively irrelevant.

Caveat emptor. Now, for all its power for organization and generalization, the abstracting process has its down side. As one climbs the ladder onto higher and higher rungs, "these new abstractions are further removed from the outside world...."[9] For instance, talking or reading *about* Pompeii, Krakatoa, or Mount St. Helen may certainly add to one's historical knowledge or scientific understanding of volcanoes, but that cannot possibly capture the cataclysm of the volcanic eruptions as actually lived (or died) through. Similarly, "freedom" as a concept or a mere slogan conveyed in a well-to-do nation long at peace would be a far cry from the sense of "freedom" earned with great personal and collective sacrifice through a brutal war and even a foreign occupation. In other words, the larger subsumptive power of higher-level abstractions is bought at the expense of decreasing familiarity with discrete experiences-in-context and lessening intimacy with people. Where generalities prevail, particularities diminish. The loss of direct contact with concrete experiences often gives rise to the sense of unintelligibility of abstract ideas, of grandiosity of theories, of vacuity of policies, and impersonality of institutions. Understandably, disillusionment is felt especially keenly in human interactions wherein a person feels that her or his uniqueness is systematically ignored through generalization, which by its nature eschews individual variations within a given category. Whenever such expressions as, "*All* adolescents are....," "*All* Spartans were ....," or "*All* schizophrenics do....," are seen or heard, we should remind ourselves of the danger of oversimplification built into the abstracting operation itself.

In the same vein, it should be kept in mind that the broader generalizability of higher-level abstractions is attained only by focusing on some select feature(s) of varied elements, while leaving out the relevant contexts as well as all other features. Once differing clusters are established, no overlaps are recognized among them, and the accompanying labeling helps to establish the difference as *factual* in our mind. The actual complexities of the person, or anything else, come to be ignored. Thus,

> If we label a person we tend to see the label, not the person. We put a label on him and then proceed to react to him as if he and all the other people so labeled were the same.... It is as if we had a word in our eye and couldn't see around it.[10]

Such pigeonholing tendencies have long been noted to underpin the stigmatization and social exclusion of the physically afflicted (including the deformed and disabled), mentally ill, intellectually divergent (e.g., the "retarded," "learning disabled," or even "gifted"), culturally different (in terms of the ethnicity, religion, language, age, occupation, social class, sexual orientation, etc.), and any other variety of "deviants." [11] Ironically, in their social ramifications, accurate diagnoses can be equally damaging as *mis*diagnoses, since the same inclusion-exclusion operation, plus labeling, can bring out the divisive, in-group vs. out-group perspective. [More will be said in Chapter 7 about the tragedies of, for instance, the Montecchi-Capuleti (i.e., Romeo-Juliet) family feud or the still prevalent idea of human "race," called by Ashley Montagu the "man's most dangerous myth."[12]]

All told, "this process of abstracting, of leaving characteristics out, is an indispensable convenience."[13] Yet, it is obvious that, in common with all other extensions, this powerful device must be handled with much care and awareness.

Analogy

Throughout our discussion, we have often referred to some familiar phrases like the *picture, portrait,* or *image* of self and the *story* or *narrative* of life. Such expressions are, of course, analogical, but the analogy is another essential extensional maneuver of nonmaterial variety that helps us in creating some order in our experiences to make better sense of it. In a nutshell, analogies use the *familiar* in our life as the means for handling the *unfamiliar*.

Let us say we are close friends with each other. One evening, after bidding farewell, I returned to my place eventlessly, but your homeward journey was interrupted when you saw some strange-looking object emitting eerie lights in a dark field nearby. Stepping out of your car to investigate, you were suddenly surrounded by several little, green creatures who, fortunately, did not appear hostile.

After a few moments of mutual hesitation, you surmised from their gestures that they were inviting you onto their "object." Being an adventurous soul that you are, you went onto that unfamiliar thing to discover that it was a flying vehicle of some sort. The ensuing spatial ride was short but spectacular, and you thoroughly enjoyed the exciting experience before your friendly hosts let you out back in the same field.

Now, what was a "short" flight for you turned out to be a week of my fear and concerns for your safety, since you seemed to have vanished without any indication of your whereabouts after that night. When you reappeared, you blithely told me that you had had a wonderful ride on a flying saucer piloted by amiable aliens. After reprimanding you for the potentially fatal recklessness, I breathlessly asked you what it was like. You tried to explain everything in detail—the spacecraft, the extraterrestrial beings, and the whole experience— without much success. Finally, out of desperation, you cried out, "Oh, it's hopeless, I cannot really describe to you what I went through. You should have been there yourself to understand! Look, so far as their flying saucer goes, it was very much like the Volkswagen Bug, the original one, you know." I said, "Oh, alright, I get you now. It isn't too big, but is well designed, right?" "Yes, that's it!" you said. "And those green creatures looked like oversized squids or something." "I see, I see," said I, without really seeing anything!

Similes. Now, this pattern of conversation is repeated endlessly in our daily life, and it reveals one of the two major categories of analogy. Notice that, in both asking questions and answering them, we cannot do without using the word, "like," or another expression of similar nature. We say, something is *like* something else, or X is *like* Y. When X is unfamiliar to the questioner, we must choose Y from among things familiar to him or her—otherwise, no sense of understanding X is induced. If, for instance, we come across "gluons"—a word unknown to many of us—and raise a question about it, such a response as, "Gluons are like quarks," would confound us as it leaves us utterly clueless about either gluons or quarks.[14]

Meanwhile, similes remain a major device by which we make sense of the cosmos, outside as well as inside of us. Indeed, many of the myriad questions young children ask can only be answered by resorting to this cultural extension: e.g., "What is an ocean?" "What is a llama?" "What is magenta?" "What is a CEO?" or "How do you open the door?" Giving only technical descriptions or definitions in response seldom helps, because they are typically even more abstract than the substance of the question. To answer more concretely, instead, with, "It is something *like* a huge pond," "It's an animal *like* a camel, smaller but with lots of hair," "Magenta looks *like* this, see?" "A CEO is the head person in a company, *like* mommy or daddy in our home," or "Do *like* this!" conveys the information the young mind needed at the moment so as to continue building his or her own scheme of comprehension. After all, there is no point in confusing and boring the child, is there?

Of course, it should be noted that, when I said in our earlier conversation about the extraterrestrials, "Oh, alright, I get you now" to you, my understanding remained at least once or twice removed from yours. You have actually seen and took a ride in "the thing," but my comprehension was based upon your verbal report given in simile. I understood the unknown flying object in terms of another machine (the old Volkswagen "Bug"), which is already in my sense-making scheme and hence known to me. Your experience was of the most direct, concrete, and indescribable variety, while mine was basically a hearsay in nature. Still, I believed I "understood," and you and I could and did carry on our communication. Knowing the unfamiliar through the familiar—that is the power of similes. Everywhere, after all, something is *like* something else.

Metaphors. While similes utilize the alleged *similarities* between X (the unknown) and Y (the known) to create an impression, at least, of comprehension, even more potent extension of metaphor claims *identity* between X and Y. Whereas the simile says "X is *like* Y," the metaphor declares "X *is* Y." Thus, all life *is* a theater, not just *like* one, and the world *is* your oyster, not merely *like* one.

This substitution of the *sameness* in metaphor for the *likeness* in simile has a sleight-of-hand character to it, since a deft switching is fully intended. "Metaphor is seeing something from the viewpoint of something else,"[15] and that "something else" can be anything whatsoever with or without any fundamental similarities to, or associations with, the "something." However, due to the suggestive juxtaposition of the "something else" with the "something," the listener or "the reader is forced to 'connect' the two ideas... In this 'connection' resides the secret and the mystery of metaphor."[16]

A different manner of looking. Indeed, the power of metaphor lies in that *conjuring up* effect on the mind, introducing a new perspective with which to look at things. When, for instance, we hear the opening line of a poem that runs, "Clouds are a genius," we are led to wonder about what the poet meant.[17] In what ways can clouds be a genius? What did he see, and what are the ramifications? All sorts of answers are possible, and each may follow a divergent line of reasoning. "If taken literally, the metaphor must be patently absurd,"[18] but the declaration of the absurd identity induces a re-examination of the familiar in an unfamiliar context. Thus, metaphor "provides a new way of understanding that which we already know, and ... reconstitutes ... new domains of perceptions and new languages of thought."[19]

Differing metaphors can certainly open up dissimilar associations and distinctive trains of thought. When Charles Darwin published in 1871 his second major work, *The Descent of Man*, [20] applying to *Homo sapiens* his thesis of natural selection expounded 20 years earlier in *On the Origin of Species*,[21] the metaphoric title in and of itself conveyed a certain message. Now, almost exactly a century later, Jacob Bronowski presented his BBC television series and a book under the title, *The Ascent of Man*,[22] referring to the process of human evolution this time via culture. Descent vs. ascent—the intended contrast in the evocations and implications could not have been clearer.

A novel metaphor opens the possibility for a shift in perspective that often triggers the "Eureka!" experience and an ensuing change in thought and action. A classic example is the dream of German chemist August Kekulé, which depicted six snakes each biting another's tail to form a ring. That was how, so goes the story, he resolved the enigma of the molecular structure of benzene (C_6H_6), consisting of only six hydrogen atoms of single valence each to go with six carbon atoms of valence four. In a similar vein, Simonton, Simonton, and Creighton, among others, reported on their pioneering application of visualization, involving iconic metaphors (i.e., in images rather than in words), in the treatment of cancer patients.[23]

> The ability to conceive of things which are not present to the senses is crucial to the development of man.... The ability to make images for absent things, and to experiment with imaginary situations, gives man a freedom which an animal does not possess.... The metaphorical images work in our minds, and shape our thought and are the essence of it....The metaphors link the different fields of our experience and seek out the likeness between them....[24]

The Unseen Lenses

As is the case with all cultural extensions, nevertheless, the power of metaphor can be less than constructive in its function. This aspect was captured nicely in the metaphor of optics when Ruth Benedict noted that, "It is hard to be conscious of the eyes through which one looks."[25] The same thought was repeated by Douglas and Ney half a century later: "The microscope itself must be our subject [of study]. The social sciences are an apparatus for seeing, and we must mark the areas that have been occluded by the equipment."[26] In other words, what enables us to see things allows us to do so only in a particular way, thus simultaneously preventing us from all other ways of seeing than the specific one.

Granted that "metaphors give shape and form to life stories,"[27] most people are not conscious of the metaphors they have been using to structure their narratives. Though new metaphors may help in "reordering experience by looking at things differently,"[28] many continue to fall back, unawares, upon the prevalent ones—for example, the "two organizing metaphors in Western thought: the journey of life metaphor and the transformation metaphor of death and rebirth."[29]

> The main point is that through these "mundane metaphors" we restrict ourselves to seeing the world in certain ways, just as with new analogies we might commit ourselves to a particular picture of the world.[30]

The restriction of our view through habituation may be seen most plainly in overworked expressions such as the *dawn* of life, the *flower* of one's youth, the *thrust* of an argument, a *shadow* of a doubt, a *lemon* of a car, or a *clarion* call, wherein metaphor has become a mere rhetorical device with little evocative power. Not surprisingly, these metaphors are called *dead* or *frozen* (metaphorically speaking, of course!).

More significant is the restriction through incognizance. To use the heart as an example, it has long been understood as a kind of *pump* that circulates the blood throughout the body. For more than three centuries, this metaphor of British royal physician William Harvey has clarified what the heart is and explained how it functions. Everybody understood that the heart *is* a pump, period. However, this simple, clear metaphor has also prevented us from seeing certain other things of relevance. If a healthy heart is seen as a machine, a ready solution recommends itself for an ailing heart—cleaning up blocked blood vessels and/or replacing any faulty parts with new or better functioning ones. Thus, in the countries like the United States, such surgical practices as angioplasty, heart bypassing, pacemaker implanting, or even heart transplanting have become established routines. However, these sorts of radical intervention have not been the uniformly preferred procedures, even within the so-called Western tradition.

For instance, the German medicine has long reflected a differing "belief that heart disease is more complex than blocked pipes," and tended to make "a diagnosis known as *Herzinsuffizienz* [cardiac insufficiency]... which would not be considered a disease in England, France, or America."[31]

> For Germans, the heart is not just a pump, but an organ that has a life of its own, one that pulsates in response to a number of different stimuli including the emotions. In other words, the German heart, as opposed to the American heart, retains some of the metaphorical associations with love and the emotions.[32]

The human body and movement. Now, as poetically put by Loren Eiseley,

> Man is, in reality, an oracular animal. Bereft of instinct, he must search constantly for meanings. We forget that, like a child, man was a reader before he became a writer, a reader of what Coleridge once called the mighty alphabet of the universe.... [33]

In its efforts to "read" the universe, the species turned, not surprisingly, to "the human body, this crown jewel of Creation," in the words of François Delsarte, which "is the universal alphabet of the encyclopedia of the world," [34] And when humans started "writing," this readily accessible alphabet was the natural choice for use. It is thus that,

> What could not yet be said in words or shaped in clay or stone, early man first danced or mimed.... In short, what André Varagnac happily identified as the "technology of the body," expressed in dance and mimetic movements, was both the earliest kind of technical order and the earliest manifestation of expressive and communicable meaning.[35]

Metaphors of body parts are everywhere: the *head* of the family, *eye* of the storm, *mouth* of a river, *jaws* of defeat, *arm* of the law, *leg* of a triangle, *foot* of the bed, and so on and so forth. More fundamentally, since all the functions of perception, conception, emotion, and action are "embodied,"[36] the body is where we start from in our attempts at sense making.

Michael Polanyi was one of the observers who acknowledged this extension character of the human body. He commented upon its usage as a tool for expression, as well as for introspection, as follows:

> Our body is the ultimate instrument of all our external knowledge, whether intellectual or practical. In all our waking moments we are *relying* on our awareness of contacts of our body with things outside for *attending* to these things. Our own body is the only thing in the world which we normally never experience as an object, but experience always in terms of the world to which we are attending from our body.[37]

Maurice Merleau-Ponty was another.

> My body is the fabric into which all objects are woven, and it is, at least in relation to the perceived world, the general instrument of my "comprehension." It is my body which gives significance not only to the natural object, but also to cultural objects like words....[38]

And, of course, there is the inimitable summation by William Butler Yeats.

> God guard me from those thoughts men think
> In the mind alone;
> He that sings a lasting song
> Thinks in a marrow-bone.[39]

It is clear that the body serves as a convenient metaphor, "a productive starting point for analyzing culture and self."[40] For instance, "in holistic sociocentric [as against egocentric] culture like India the human body, conceived as an inter-dependant system, is frequently taken as a metaphor for society.... [as] a model of differentiated parts arranged in a hierarchy of functions in the service of the whole."[41]

Now, granted that the body may be a good metaphorical tool for many applications, how have we been making sense of the human body itself, this familiar, yet mysterious, keystone of life?[42] What metaphors have we typically used to decipher the nature of this "instrument" per se? It appears that there are enough simple-minded ones like, "Old age is but the reduced capacity of a failing machine."[43] However, it is instructive to read that, after exploring the views of the body as a beast of burden, as a machine, an "objet d'art," and a child, Carol-Lynne Moore was led to entertain a more inclusive, if elusive, one of the body as a chimera, a fire-spitting monster of Greek mythology comprising the parts of a few differing animals, hence difficult to capture in a simple, single way.[44]

Similarly, when the movement of the whole body across space and time is considered, none of the prevailing metaphors appears to capture the full scope and complexity of movement in all its functions and contexts.[45] Language, whether seen as universal, foreign, or idiosyncratic, provides a metaphor that is atomistic, linear, causal, and rule-bound. However, it tends to obscure the wholistic, multidimensional, synchronic, and intuitive aspects of movement, which may be highlighted by the metaphor of painting. Meanwhile, the synthesis of synchronicity and sequentiality revealed in movement may suggest music as a more appropriate metaphor.

Admittedly, each of these metaphors offers its useful perspective, but there appear to have been strangely few attempts to explicate the full ramifications and implications of any of them. Thus, in many ways, the prevalent metaphors of human movement remain iconic in character. Unlike "analogic metaphors," which arranges "words or frames in a linear series," iconic metaphors present "a unique and unparaphrasable image" in "a single... auto-referential frame,"[46] that is to say, an intuitive bird's-eye view. However, "no effective metaphor ... can be entirely iconic or analogic"[47]—there have to be both varieties in any formal attempts at comprehension and application. As in all creative efforts, original insights must be followed up, scrutinized, and further developed for fruition.

In trying to decipher the complexity of human movement, it is likely that the iconic metaphor for its spatial structure needs to be integrated with the analogic metaphor for its melodic structure. In the spatial category, the polygons more familiar in solid geometry and crystallography may prove helpful, according to the explorations by, among others, Leonardo da Vinci [48] and Rudolf von Laban.[49] In the melodic category, on the other hand, the harmonic scales of music could be a fruitful metaphor. In fact, according to Carol-Lynne Moore,[50] the unifying principles of proportion, connection, and harmony were already embodied in Laban's treatises of the "choreutics" (the study of *statics*, dealing with the structure, form, and potential) and the "eukinetics" (the study of *dynamics* that has to do with the function, action, and kinetics) of movement. It appears that Laban was seeking to develop a "theoretical model" in which the felt need for extending the original domain, in this case the movement study, was fulfilled by drawing upon the corpus of knowledge and conjecture in,

> a more familiar, or better-organized secondary domain.... Inferences from the assumptions made in the secondary field are translated by means of the [explicit or implicit] rules of correlation and then independently checked against known or predicted data in the primary domain.... [T]he key to understanding the entire transaction is the identity of structure that in favorable cases permits assertions made about the secondary domain to yield insight into the original field of interest.[51]

Though relying on the same operational principle of "pour[ing] new content into old bottles," theoretical models go beyond commonplace metaphors in suggesting further hypotheses for inquiry, due to the twin requirements of the "systematic complexity of the source of the model and capacity for analogical development."[52] Yet, both simple metaphors and systematic models ultimately hinge upon "an implicit or submerged model in a writer's thought," often called the "root metaphors."[53]

Root Metaphor

The root metaphor is the comprehensive, organizing analogy that helps in making sense of experiences, interpreting the world, and defining the meaning of life. "We might say that root metaphors describe worlds, while models describe the contents of those worlds."[54]

Is the whole universe a perfect machine? Is the society an organism? Is the planet Earth itself alive [as in the Gaia hypothesis[55]]? Is life a long, arduous journey? Is the present a phase in the fateful karmic cycle? Is social interaction a game? Though mostly implicit, a large set of assumptions stems out of each of such root metaphors to form one's *Weltanschauung*.

That fundamental world view is the "lenses" of Benedict and the "microscope" of Douglas and Ney [quoted at the beginning of the preceding section], which will skew what people see as *the* reality and, even unawares, will affect their judgments, mood, and conduct in all aspects of living. Certainly, life will look very differently to a person whose metaphor is that of a ruthless, gladiatorial combat to the bitter end than to another who perceives an aspen grove wherein each tree grows individually while sustained by a common network of roots. Accordingly, the two lives will be lived very differently. Life seen as a cathedral to be built, as the gambling game of craps, or as the oyster that creates pearl out of an irritant grain of sand—each presupposition generates its own script for life.

Needless to say, a collective life can be similarly influenced by some commonly held root metaphors, and a whole generation, organization, community, nation, continent, or even world may appear to fall under the spell of the so-called *Zeitgeist* [the spirit of the age] to reveal certain, particular perspectives, ideas, sentiments, attitudes, or practices. For example, quite a few manufacturing terms sneak into the discussion of schooling to reflect how many people think of the process as a matter of production and marketing. They thus speak of the need for better input management (i.e., student recruitment), output specifications (behavioral objectives), quality control (mass testing), customer feedback (student satisfaction), product sales (placement of graduates), and the like.[56] In a similar vein, it is quite noticeable that many business talks and everyday news reports are couched in military phrasing, e.g., "Target the up-market by bulleting the main points," "Deploy your heavy guns in an aggressive sales campaign," "This is the last line of our defense," "The loss this quarter has been heavy, let's retreat and regroup," "The population increase is the real time bomb here," "Soldiers of the Lord are on the march," "Dolphins torpedo Jets," "Toyota's stealth attack on Honda," etc. The point is that such casual expressions and remarks reflect the outlook stemming from the underlying root metaphor.

Two divided cultures? "Abstract concepts are largely metaphorical,"[57] and "all theories are metaphoric,"[58] *no matter where they are found.* However, many of us forget this, and believe that metaphors are matters of significance mostly in arts and humanities, not in mundane life and certainly not in *exact* or hard sciences. Needless to say, many statements have been made on the subject of arts and humanities *versus* sciences. The view of two radically divided cultures[59] is still widespread, and some explications, even by knowledgeable authors, can themselves be rather misleading. Let us look at two sample declarations.

> Often it is the poet who grasps these matters [human thoughts] most firmly and concisely. The elegant rationality of science and the metaphoric nonrationality of art operate with deeply different grammars; perhaps they even represent a profound complementarity. For in the experience of art, we connect by a grammar of metaphor.[60]

> I have no doubt now that there is a common quality in science and in poetry—the quality of imagination. But I have no doubt either ... that ... the imagination reaches us, reaches into us, in different ways in science and in poetry.... It is the poet's images that set off our own imagination.... In this sense, all art is metaphor.[61]

Granted certain pertinence of each such observation, it must by now be recognized that, fundamentally, "it is only by the hook of the analogy, by the root metaphor..., that science succeeds in extending its domain."[62] Indeed, in sciences, which are allegedly quite precise, "the use of models ... has strongly resembled the use of metaphors" in humanities and arts.[63] Theoretical models of science, "as a more general kind of metaphor," resort to the same "metaphorical thought [as] a distinctive mode of achieving insight."[64] And the shift of "paradigms"[65] in scientific revolution is the changing of root metaphors by an imaginative leap. Thus, although "the imaginative aspects of scientific thought have in the past been too much neglected..., [the] exercise of the imagination ... [in fact] provides a common ground"[66] for all human mentation.

Fundamentally, therefore, *how* we think does not vary with *what* we think about. Irrespective of the *what*, "metaphors, deliberately selected to guide our thinking, ... have generalized effects on how we think."[67] Moreover, regardless of the contents of the specific metaphor so chosen, the metaphorical maneuver itself hinges upon seeing one thing *as if* it were something else, which in fact it is *not*. "The metaphor lies not in the thing seen ... but in the stance of the see-er, his standing within one picture, so to speak, in order to attain a certain vision of another."[68] That vision may be crystal clear and so patently true to the particular observer. Still, when one's sight is expanded too far afield, that convincing perspective ceases to be functional. "Metaphors ... serve as rhetorical forestructures through which the observational world is construed.... Each [metaphor] carries with it certain advantages and limitations ... and each constructs a different ontology."[69]

Thus, no matter how powerful and inclusive it might appear, any given metaphor, paradigm, or theory is by nature a device of limited application, not a universal solution to every puzzle. In that sense, its utility lies in its tentativeness and, if reified, its usefulness is over.

Notes

1. Gergen, 1991, 165.
2. Korzybski, 1948, 424.
3. Hayakawa, 1964.
4. Apparently, the medical prescriptions may be filled only in the "Apotheke," while the "Drogerie" is where substances of alternative medicine are found. Both handle typical non-prescriptive medications, as well as toiletries, etc., and both are usually clustered together under the "Pharmazie" at the next higher abstraction level. Meanwhile, the "charcuterie" is where one looks specifically for pork meat and its derivative products such as ham, sausage, and paté, whereas the "boucherie" refers to a more general butcher shop (which can thus be a level higher on the ladder of abstraction). Finally, the "minicab" represents the taxi-ing service by independent operators whose private automobiles are run without a taximeter. Accordingly, it is advisable to agree on the fee beforehand.
5. Hayakawa, 1964, 217.
6. Piaget, 1976.
7. Korzybski, 1948, 39.
8. Ibid., 291.
9. Ibid.
10. W. Johnson and Moeller, 1972, 67-68.
11. E.g., H. Becker, 1966; Goffman, 1963; Mercer, 1973; Murphy, 1990; Scheff, 1999.
12. Montagu, 1998.
13. Hayakawa, 1964, 180.
14. Apparently, "gluons" is the name assigned to the elementary particles now believed to make up the "quarks" (a word borrowed from James Joyce's *Finnegans Wake*), which are, in turn, hypothesized to make up protons and neutrons in the atom's nucleus, surrounded by electrons. Earlier, it may be recalled, atom was believed to be of a piece, being the smallest, indivisible building unit of the universe. In contrast, the current view of the structural features of the universe is somewhat remindful of (i.e., "like") the colorfull Russian dolls of wood that successively encase the next smaller one.
15. R. Brown, 1989, 77.
16. Black, 1962, 39.
17. The celebrated Japanese poet was Takuboku Ishikawa (1885-1920).
18. R. Brown, 1989, 81.
19. Ibid., 98.
20. Darwin, 1871.
21. Darwin, 1859.

22. Bronowski, 1981
23. Simonton, Matthews-Simonton, and Creighton, 1978.
24. Bronowski, 1978, 9, 11, 15.
25. Benedict, 1946, 14.
26. Douglas and Ney, 1998, xiv.
27. G. Becker, 1999, 188.
28. Ibid., 177.
29. Ibid., 184.
30. Sanford, 1987, 55.
31. Payer, 1989, 81.
32. Ibid., 80.
33. Eiseley, 1969, 144.
34. Porte, 1992, xi.
35. Mumford, 1967, 62.
36. Lakoff and Johnson, 1999.
37. Polanyi, 1967, 15.
38. Merleau-Ponty, 1962, 235.
39. Yeats, 1950.
40. Csordas, 1990, 39.
41. Shweder and LeVine, 1984, 191.
42. An appropriate reminder comes from a distinguished British doctor, Fellow of the Royal Society, and Professor at the University of Oxford, Sir. David Weatherall, 2002: "Human beings are unbelievably complex organisms about which we understand very little." This observation of his was also reported by Gearin-Tosh, 2002.
43. Jackson, 1997, 4.
44. Moore, 1987. See, also, Moore, 1992.
45. Moore and Yamamoto, 1988.
46. R. Brown, 1989, 85, 86.
47. Ibid., 88.
48. Panofsky, 1940.
49. Laban, 1974.
50. Moore, 2003; Moore, 2005.
51. Black, 1962, 230-231.
52. Ibid., 239.
53. Pepper, 1942.
54. R. Brown, 1989, 126.
55. Lovelock, 1979.
56. Yamamoto, 1993.
57. Lakoff and Johnson, 1999, 3.
58. R. Brown, 1989, 99.
59. Snow, 1959.
60. Bruner, 1962a, 74.

61. Bronowski, 1978, 5, 15, 16.
62. Eiseley, 1980, 20.
63. Black, 1962, 236.
64. Ibid., 237.
65. Kuhn, 1962.
66. Black, 1962, 243.
67. Shweder and LeVine, 1984, 193.
68. R. Brown, 1989, 128.
69. Gergen, 1997, 41-42.

Chapter 7. Wayfarers, Beware!

When the humanity is examined through the lens of cultural extensions, one may get the impression of watching the legendary King Midas of Phrygia. A mighty monarch, he was even accorded by Dionysus the special power to turn everything he touched to gold. Alas, that marvel ended tragically when he embraced his beloved daughter into a gold statue of a girl. Of course, this is the same king who suffered the ignominy of sporting large ears of ass after blindly favoring the inferior but familiar god, Pan, over Apollo in a musical contest he had judged.

For all the exciting feats through its history, *Homo* appears to have been paying dearly for its special potential by not fully understanding the nature of its clever creations. Certainly, all sorts of extensions have provided it with increasing power for some proud accomplishments, but also for some notable infamies. The species' trails have been marked by many dead ends, and the same errors of judgment seem to have been committed generation after generation.

Long Detours via Alleged Shortcuts

It may be fairly said that one triad, among others, describes the features cherished in contemporary America and many other industrialized cultures. The three elements are speed, convenience, and comfort. Ideas, inventions, or devices that help save time, labor, and physical malaise are much in demand, and it is typically argued that the combined savings will bring an improvement in physical and financial conditions and a better life style, both individually and collectively. As is the case with all extensions, however, the alleged shortcuts for such attractive goals often lead us astray, revealing the self-defeating, shadow side of the endeavor.

Habits, routines, and customs. For instance, everyone develops some habits and certain routines in daily life. Their origins may be an obscure happenstance, but the particular manners of individual expression, gesture, posture, locomotion, efforts, tempo, etc., as well as the specific approaches to the tasks and chores at hand, are adopted and sustained in the belief, at least, of their efficacy as an aid for attaining some personal or social ends. When a child, did we not refuse *with conviction* anything green in our diet? Was it the rule to eat our favorite food on the plate first, or to save it for the very last bite? Did we always run through a scary part of our neighborhood? As an adult, do we put our socks or stockings on first or last in dressing? Are there not some special suits, ties, dresses, shoes, or accessories we always wear for certain occasions? Do we take the same train or bus every day to and from work, or drive a car following the same route? Do we resort to some stock quips, jokes, or stories to "break the ice"?

Personal tastes, preferences, and attitudes are similarly developed within the confines of organismic-ecological givens and social contexts, which include the cultural taboos, mores, and customs. Ordinarily, we are unlikely to consider these constructions as extensions, but we are forced to acknowledge their life-organizng powers when our familiar routines are disrupted by such radical events as accident, illness, death, natural or man-made disaster, emigration, or even childbirth. Far more benign experiences like foreign travels may be enough to remind us how easily we can get disoriented and incapacitated in situations wherein our regular habits, routines, and customs not only "do not work" any longer but may also generate personal discomfiture and social conflicts. In addition to the typical difficulties in the linguistic realm, one is faced with unfamiliar foodstuff, unheard-of brands of cosmetic and pharmaceutical products, different cuts and sizing of clothing items, and so on. *Routine* hand gestures, *innocuous* body postures, *common* moves, *ordinary* vocalizations, or *usual* outfit may take on quite different, unintended meanings to give rise to mutual misunderstandings, or even worse.

In such circumstances, one may suddenly realize that there are indeed no such thing as innocuous, common habits, or ordinary, usual routines, or universal, everyday conventions. The interactive "action chain" cannot be readily forged because its "steps and stages are unique for each culture"[1] and, besides, the governing rules remain in the domain of the non-explicit "cultural unconscious" to make outsiders' learning very difficult.[2] "In fact, they [action chains] have not been cataloged [*sic*], nor has a preliminary list been made even for a single culture."[3]

The tacit nature of the *proper* practice is well reflected in, among many other examples, the initial fright and consternation we experience in pedestrian-driver or driver-driver interactions when visiting, say, the United Kingdom or Japan. Needless to say, people drive on the right-hand side of the road in the U.S., while the Britons and Japanese do so on the left. It takes quite a while before the visitors can, unerringly and quickly, look in the correct directions in crossing the street or glance up into the rear-view mirror. Some years back, an acquaintance of mine, who had gone to London to study with a master teacher in her profession, reported back to us, recounting her many close encounters with automobiles. "I am still having trouble figuring out which way to look before stepping into a crosswalk," wrote she. "The day before yesterday, I came so, so close to be run over by a car turning left around a corner real fast at an intersection. Honestly, I really thought I had had it this time. You will think it funny but, in that split second, I saw a big, brown dog driving the car, and that terrified me even more!!"[4] Familiar routines are as comfortable and convenient as a pair of old sheepskin boots, but their usefulness is situational in nature. When we forget that, the nice features lull us to complacence and inertia, and we become immune to the new and different. We thus make ourselves less than educable and changeable. In the words of Wendell Johnson:

> I am not unaware of the discomfort of learning…. We are a lot like the pilot in
> training who is learning to fly by instrument. The only way he can do this is to

do what feels wrong. I think this is one of the best definitions of education I have ever heard: If what we are saying and what we are doing do not feel a little wrong, in that sense then, we are not learning. We are not changing. We are just doing what we are used to doing. And that is not education.[5]

Cognitive shortcuts of heuristics. The routines people use in the mental realm are formally named "heuristics." These are "cognitive shortcuts," which "people use to judge probabilities and to make decisions under uncertain circumstances."[6] There are all sorts of such devices we habitually apply in quickly figuring out what is going on now, whether some event will come to pass, how valuable something might be, who can be trusted, and so on and so forth. A few among them are quite common.

For example, people often mistake me, a person of Japanese heritage, for a Chinese. Since they are not sure who I really am, they fall back upon what they are, or *believe* they are, familiar with, and make up their mind. In other words, I may look or act *just like* a Chinese [as *they* understand it], and that stereotype is sufficient for the particular classification. I personify all the characteristics of Chinese-ness known to them, so they use what is called the *representativeness heuristics*. Likewise, a friend of mine, who is originally from a Middle Eastern country, a graduate of a major American university, and one of the top-notch insurance executives in the United States, continues to be identified as a Muslim, when he is in fact a Christian. It is easy to see how the use of this heuristics, though convenient for many purposes, can easily lead to bias and injustice. Obviously, therefore, such instrument as the "passenger profiles," which has been in use by security forces in most major airports for identification of potential terrorists among the passengers, must be based upon a better representativeness of the featured appearance-conduct indexes and upon their higher discriminant validity than in our mundane shortcuts.

Another common mental routine is called the *availability heuristics* wherein people decide on the basis of information most easily recalled or most readily available. For example, many magazine or newspaper advertisements make a point of including the phrase, "As seen on TV," as alleged guarantee of the quality of their products. In fact, of course, such an attribute has nothing to do with the actual quality of whatever they are trying to sell. To many potential buyers, nevertheless, the television commercial may have been the only source of information available for arriving at judgment. It is not even necessary for them to have actually watched the broadcast—the claim of such a TV advertisement suffices to plant or revive the brand or company name in the consumers' mind. The mental shortcut does the rest.

Similarly, parents, teachers, and coaches are prone to expect, at least implicitly, from new children or students the capability and performance similar to that shown earlier by their older siblings. In the same vein, those whose names are readily recognizable, be they politicians, entertainers, business establishments, mercantile products, shows and movies, or publications benefit (or suffer) from this publicity shortcut. For the same reason, younger generations of medical and veterinary professionals, who did not grow up with such dreaded diseases as bubonic plague, tuberculosis, poliomyelitis, hoof-and-mouth, or anthrax may not immediately detect their early symptoms for the lack of direct, or even second-hand, experience with them.

Another heuristic is named the *anchoring and adjustment*, and refers again to our basic tendency to derive judgment first from our tried and true experience (which is our anchor, or main reference) and then adjust it later, if at all, this way or that way. A good example is the first impressions we form of people, places, etc. As we know, they are a really powerful anchor in many instances, and we are unwilling to make any adjustments to them even when warranted!

Another example is the preoccupation, when people first travel overseas, to convert every foreign price to its equivalent in their own currency. Understandably, the prices we would have paid at home for similar merchandises, meals, transportation, or service become the natural anchor for most of us, but the results seldom serve as a good guide for the actual purchasing power of the unfamiliar money within its own market structure. The judgment of where to spend and where to economize in the new environment calls for quite a bit of adjustments to the *virtual* reality created by a simple conversion. Similarly, as a personal example, when we moved to the U.K. for our temporary assignments, we estimated the time it should take to drive from *A* to *B* by first converting the distance from kilometers to miles, then dividing it with, let's say, 45 or 50 (miles an hour). This scheme, which had been reasonable for us in the western U.S., did not work too well, given the narrow, serpentine roads without any shoulders; typically rainy, windy weather; unfamiliar road signs (like those painted on the road surface); perennially heavy traffic; and, of course, the confusing (to us) left-sided traffic. Needless to say, we were rapidly forced to change our formula and curtail our ambition for rapid displacement.

Yet another common variety of cognitive shortcuts bears the name, *simulation heuristics,* in which a person conjures up a likely or desired scenario of an event to come, and act according to the plot. In essence, this is the same process as the writing and living of the story of life, discussed earlier in Chapter 5. As noted there, different stories can fit the same particulars, some being cogent and inspiring while others incoherent and demoralizing. Either way, the storyteller is inclined to live his or her story of choice.

Not surprisingly, observers have noticed such heuristics in, among other applications, how judges arrive at their sentences in trying criminal defendants.

> As judges gather information about a case, they weave it into a coherent story with temporal and causal relationships.... Judges compose the stories by using their understanding of the events and the people in the case.... Furthermore, differences result from variations in the kinds of stories judges prefer.... This

process also suggests why it would be difficult to change a judge's mind about a case—it involves unravelling a lot of the story and undoing a complicated and time-consuming creative effort."[7]

There have been other judgment heuristics identified and studied,[8] but they all share the features common to any cultural extensions. They are convenient and useful, but they can also easily lead us astray unless we remain alert to the down side of their power. For instance, examining the possibilities for improving heuristics for clinical decision making in medicine and discussing the "expert systems [which] are computer programs that solve problems and give advice by making inferences from the available data," Steven Schwartz had this to say: "One important goal of many clinical expert systems is to suggest hypotheses that might otherwise go unconsidered.... On the negative side, compared with human experts, expert systems often display an amazing lack of common sense. This is known as the 'plateau and cliff' effect. Programs perform well in a circumscribed problem area, but once they are asked to perform outside their limited domain, there is not a graceful decline but rather a sudden and dramatic drop in performance."[9] One notices here a restatement of the "spill-over effects" of cultural extensions mentioned earlier [Chapter 3].

In the end, therefore, what promises to be a shortcut can turn out a long detour or even a dead end for unwary travellers.

Lost and Confused

There is a popular expression that says, "My mind is playing a trick on me." That, interestingly, is exactly how non-material extensions often work to lead us astray unless we are *mindful!* As we noted in our earlier discussion of the abstraction process [Chapter 6], the mind categorizes particulars, labels them, and classifies them into a hierarchical ladder in our attempts to comprehend the world and our experiences therein. "The [typical] classification system is an excellent example of how the majority of ... people has been trained to think.... The result has been ... that ... we find ourselves deeply preoccupied with specifics ... to the exclusion of everything else.... Where do we go for the overview?"[10]

Being stuck on the ladder. To arrive at the overall picture, one must move about the whole ladder of abstraction to assume varied viewpoints. However, many of us cannot or will not so move and rather stay put on only certain rungs. If a person is used to, and felt more comfortable at, more concrete levels of operation, he or she may exhibit the literal mindedness of some favorite caricature characters. For instance, hearing her friend say, "Alright, let's hit the road," Amelia Bedelia.would promptly go outside and start striking the road surface with a stick. Likewise, if told by Asterix to "Throw out the net now!," Obelix would chuck the whole fishing net clear overboard without securing the end. Or, Zero is commanded by angry Sergent Snorkel, "Pardon my French, but tell those guys to get that [expletives] ditch dug!," and slowly walks over with a shovel in hand to where

Beetle Baily and others are goofing off in a half-finished ditch. When Beetle asks him, "What did Sarge say?," Zero answers, "I dunno. It was in French."[11]

We come across many such people who perennially operate with a more concrete orientation in everyday interactions. For example, kind locals have often given me such directions as, "The Post Office? Ah ... yes, stay on this road until the corner where the old school house used to be. Turn left there, and then turn right when you see a big oak tree. It's easy, you can't miss it!" As another example, here is a fascinating interchange between a clerk and a client I once overheard in a governmental agency.

> Clerk: "I have to put down your birthplace on this form. Where were you born?
> Client: "Home."
> Clerk: "Home, yeah, but where?"
> Client: "In the bedroom."
> Clerk: "No, no, where, the place—like the town, you know?"
> Client: "Oh, yes, in town." [You can guess the rest!]

Not unexpectedly, those who are used to stay down on the abstraction ladder and remain on the more concrete rungs would find it difficult to engage in games and exercises like "Just Suppose," "Let's Pretend," "Can You Imagine?" or "What If?" that require one to come up with alternative ideas and explore potential courses of action.

In contrast, there are obviously numerous others who are inclined to stay on the more abstract end of the ladder. The "absent-minded professors" epitomize these people, but they may also be easily found in all walks of life. In fact, the increasing specialization tends to restrict many a professional to a limited range on the upper rungs and to make them refuse or unable to benefit from the full view. As a result, for all their expertise and erudition, they may miss the whole picture, thus ironically joining the concrete-minded at the other end. "It is obvious, then, that interesting speech and interesting writing, as well as clear thinking and psychological well-being, require the constant interplay of higher- and lower-level abstractions, and the constant interplay of the verbal [i.e., abstract] levels with the nonverbal ("object" [or concrete]) levels."[12]

Another way of saying this is that the desirable "overview" in the Hall quotation above [Footnote 10] requires two kinds of awareness in a delicate balance.

> Skilful knowing and doing is performed by subordinating a set of particulars, as clues or tools, to the shaping of a skilful achievement.... We may then be said to become "subsidiarily aware" of these particulars within our "focal awareness" of the coherent entity that we achieve.... All particulars become meaningless if we lose sight of the pattern which they jointly constitute.... When focusing on a whole, we are subsidiarily aware of its parts, while there is no difference in the intensity of the two kinds of awareness.[13]

All in all, it is not a good idea to get stuck on any specific rungs on a given abstraction ladder.

At the same time, it is not a good idea either to get stuck with any particular ladder of choice. Because the abstracting process itself hinges as much upon exclusion as upon inclusion [see Chapter 6], we must remember that multiple ladders can be constructed from the same concrete elements. "In simple words, we obtain similarities by disregarding differences, by a process of abstracting."[14] Which differences are to be ignored to establish which similarities?—that is the abstracter's decision. Granted there may be a temporarily fashionable, collectively imposed way (sometimes characterized as "received" or "politically correct") to cluster and label the elements in a specific realm of life, no scheme of classification is God-given to claim an immutable, universal advantage. Think, for example, of the identification of the Census ethnicity, categorization of political persuasions, establishment of tax brackets, diagnosis of psychiatric and medical conditions, assignment of course grades, viewer suitability rating of movies, quality ranking of securities and corporations, and so on.

It should be remembered that "the [seemingly self-evident] division of nature into inanimate and animate and intrapsychic realms is strictly the product of Western European thinking. Other cultures carve up the universe differently."[15] In other words, no abstraction scheme pre-empts the *reality*, and no single, fixed approach is suitable for all tasks in all circumstances. Versatility to take into account the nature of the *task* at hand in the specific *context* thus becomes a virtue.

Staying confounded on the ladder*.* Meanwhile, even on a particular ladder, confusion is easy to arise when differing levels of abstraction are confounded with each other.

> If, through lack of consciousness of abstracting, we identify or confuse words with objects and feelings, or memories and "ideas" with experiences which belong to the un-speakable objective level, we identify higher order abstractions with lower.[16]

This has been called the "'Is' of identity" trap, and Alfred Korzybski further pointed out that, "Say whatever you choose *about* the object, and whatever you might say *is not* it," or, "Whatever you might *say* the object 'is', well it *is not*."[17]

Table 7-1. Some Worthy Reminders

Map	=/=	Territory
Word	=/=	Thing
Extensions	=/=	Human Beings
Self-Concept	=/=	Self
Story of Life	=/=	Life

A set of formulae in Table 7-1 expresses this reminder for the purposes of our discussion.

The caution is doubly pertinent in handling metaphors. As examined in Chapter 6, the power of metaphor lies in its *as if* feature which, however, is easily overlooked to make us believe what a metaphor depicts as the *reality*. There is a large difference between noting that "X is *like* Y" (simile) and declaring that "X *is* Y" (metaphor). The latter is an example of the "'Is' of identity."

When applied to oneself or to any others, the forgotten difference between the two analogic expressions becomes significant in its implications. For instance, it is one thing to admonish a child, "That's enough. You are now behaving *like* a bad boy," while it is another to assert, "Stop it! You *are* a bad boy." Likewise, there is quite a contrast between admitting that every one of us sometimes acts *like* an idiot and branding someone to *be* a total idiot for all times and under any circumstances. While similes allow for relative, situational descriptions of a person's conduct or features, metaphors (with the built-in "'is' of identity") lead to an absolute character typing, touching upon the quintessence of the individual. That is the reason why it is important to keep the distinction clearly in mind. One of those who put this reminder into action was the Austrian pioneer in youth work, August Aichhorn,[18] who influenced Sigmund Freud among others. He made it very clear to the youngsters under his guidance that, while he loved them as persons, he did not care for and condone their anti-social and self-defeating behaviors.

Still, even keener minds among us have not successfully avoided the abstraction trap. Black tells the story of the two great, 19th century British physicists, Clark Maxwell and Lord Thomson Kelvin. The two offered quite contrasting interpretations as regards the imponderable substance, ether.

> There is certainly a vast difference between treating the ether as a mere heuristic convenience, as Maxwell's first remarks require, and treating it in Kelvin's fashion as "real matter" having definite ... properties independent of our imagination. The difference is between thinking of the electrical field *as if* it were filled with a material medium, and thinking of it *as being* such a medium. One approach uses a detached comparison reminiscent of simile and argument from analogy; the other requires an identification typical of metaphor.[19]

The more powerful a cultural extension is, the more mindful we must be of the nature of that power. In the present case, "that metaphor retain its consciously 'as if' quality is ... a pivotal point, for on it turns the difference between using metaphors and being used by them"[20]

Single perspectives. In our discussion on the image of self [Chapter 5], it was pointed out that the self-concept never exhausts the self. That is to say, no matter how thoroughly we describe ourselves in response to the question, "Who am I?", the depicted *me* cannot convey everything about the *I*, the being who is doing the describing. The "*I* am *me*" statement can tell a lot, but it cannot tell all about the person herself or himself, the one who is coming up with the particular details. The image, concept, or story of self is indeed a powerful extension, but it is never the self itself (see Table 7-1). Alas, this fact escapes most of us many times, and we try hard to "live up to" the somewhat fictional characters of our own creation and/or of others' expectation. Thus, the subject (i.e., ourselves, the agent) is reduced to the object .

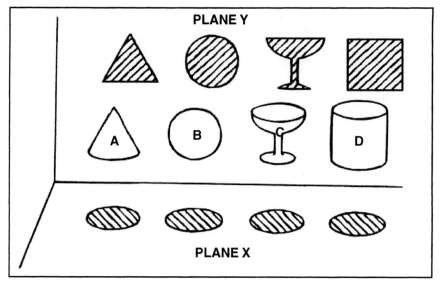

Figure 7-1. Perspectives and Perceptions

In Korzybski's expression, "Nature is inexhaustible; the events have infinite numbers of characteristics...," whereas our "acquaintance [is] *specific* and *partial*."[21] For example, witnesses can give very different accounts of the same incident, depending upon where they happened to be. Even the same person's observations can vary according to their changing points of view, literally or figuratively. "It is difficult to get the complete picture out of fractional ones.... From one perspective, all [the objects] may look alike when they are actually radically different [Figure 7-1; compare the projections on plane X]. From another perspective, however, images may appear to be very different, when they are in fact of the same object [Figure 7-1; compare, for each object, the two projections on planes X and Y].[22]

Hence, we must accept what Korzybski called the principle of "non-allness." We cannot become acquainted with anything in all its multitudinous aspects by any chosen means at any given time and space. Exhaustiveness is beyond our ken, and the prevalent belief in the one-and-only, exclusive reality is not supportable. Nevertheless, the know-it-all-ness persists and the exclusivity of reasoning unfortunately abounds. "Reductionism" is a case in point, which is "the tendency to think that understanding results from reducing complex phenomena to their simplest elements, or to a single basic principle of explanation."[23]

As for the first-named tendency of reductionism above, "the implicit assumption [therein is] that the smaller and more isolable the units into which phenomena can be broken down the clearer and more precise specifications can be, and the closer we can come to reality. It is this implicit assumption that has characterized much of the development of Western science and that is currently open to question."[24] What typically ensues is this: "one breaks the whole up into parts; and as always happens when one separates the part from the whole ... one magnifies the tiny part, making it ridiculously important, so that no one may notice that the tiny part is not the whole."[25]

> Taken alone, [the reductionistic approach] may or may not be judged successful.... The real trouble, nevertheless, rests with the fact that nothing can be "taken alone" in organic matter without its losing significance.... Separate parts can be analyzed to death, but no understanding of the whole would come from such examination. In living human beings, we are dealing with the whole, not with this or that trait, or even with one hundred traits side by side. What are the secrets of synthesis? That is the query never answered by the reigning reductionism in social and behavioral science.[26]

To repeat the point, "the belief that, since particulars are more tangible, their knowledge offers a true conception of things is fundamentally mistaken.... Scrutinize closely the particulars of a comprehensive entity and their meaning is effaced, our conception of the entity is destroyed."[27] A part of the difficulty rests with the fact that "the operations of a higher level cannot be accounted for by the laws governing its particulars forming the lower level."[28]

Now, as noted above [Footnote 23], the alternative tendency of reductionism is "to think that understanding results from reducing complex phenomena ... to a single basic principle of explanation." American behaviorism of John B. Watson, B. F. Skinner, and many others may epitomize this perspective. So do also theories of cultural homogeneity of "the reductionists—Marxists, neoclassical economists, cultural materialists, orthodox Freudians, and sociobiologists—whose basic premises include uniformities of structure and content in human life, culture, and motivation at all times and places. They are inclined to minimize cultural variability and to interpret evidence of variations as surface manifestations concealing the deeper uniformities forecast by their theoretical positions."[29] The basic trouble with the whole orientation is that "the effort to achieve what seems to be logical completeness, valuable as it is for some purposes, may lead to neglect of the full subtleties and complexities of important experiences."[30]

Another manifestation of "the fallacy of reductionism, a nothing-but way of thinking" is found in the frequent "ignoring of the necessity of historical analysis for understanding of human behavior, and of the extent to which what we call human nature is the product of a concrete historical situation."[31] This oversight seems all the more ironic because it is practiced by humans,[32] the very beings whose peculiarity was summarized by Ortega y Gasset as follows:

> *Man, in a word, has no nature; what he has* [instead] *is ... history.* Expressed differently: what nature is to things, history ... is to man."[33]

A relevant reminder was offered also by Jacob Bronowski.

> Of course, it is tempting—very tempting to a scientist—to hope that the most original achievements of the mind are also the most recent.... Yet to admire only our own successes, as if they had no past (and were sure of the future), would make a caricature of knowledge.[34]

It is for this very reason that some have called to our attention the fact that "progress was often achieved by a 'criticism from the past'.... The whole history of a subject is [to be] utilized in the attempt to improve its most recent and most 'advanced' stage."[35]

Not surprisingly, reductionism is no stranger to "fanaticism, enthusiasm ... hatred and intolerance [since] all of them demand blind faith and singlehearted allegiance." To *the true believer* so characterized by Hoffer, "to live without an ardent dedication is to be adrift and abandoned." However, the principles and programs of a particular creed matter far less to the person than the fact of fervent involvement in some mass movement that is "uncompromising, intolerant, proclaiming the one and only truth." So, "[the fanatic] embraces a cause not primarily because of its justness and holiness but because of his desperate need for something to hold on to. Often, indeed, it is his need for passionate attachment which turns every cause he embraces into a holy cause."[36]

Because of this zealous adherence to, and even the "readiness to die"[37] for, the doctrinal authority, be it philosophical, religious, political, or social in nature, various beliefs within the "closed mind" remain isolated and un-integrated. Ironically, therefore, such "a party-line thinker is a person who not only resists change but can also change only too easily. What he does depends on what his authorities do, and his changes and refusals conform with authority."[38] In fact, "where mass movements are in violent competition with each other, there are not infrequent instances of converts—even the most zealous—shifting their allegiance from one to the other. A Saul turning into Paul is neither a rarity nor a miracle."[39]

The Ways of Reasoning

Obviously, it is hard to be cognizant of the influence of what one's mind has created, especially in the category of the nonmaterial extensions. Culture is to humans what water is to the fish — both are too close and hermetic to allow much chance for a view from the outside. "Culture equips each of us with built-in blinders, hidden and unstated assumptions that control our thoughts and block the unraveling of cultural processes."[40] In fact, "every society excludes certain thoughts and feelings from being thought, felt, and expressed." Through the *"socially conditioned filter"* of language, logic, and experiential content , culture regulates what may or may not enter into our awareness and how to handle each. "Generally speaking," for instance, "it may be said that an experience rarely comes into awareness for which the language has no word."[41]

The same dynamics applies to logic. "Just as most people assume that their language is 'natural'... they assume also that the rules which determine proper thinking are natural and universal ones; that what is illogical in one cultural system is illogical in any other, because it conflicts with 'natural' logic."[42] Patently, neither assumption holds, since "there are many different and legitimate ways of thinking; we in the West value one of these ways above all others—the one we call 'logic,' a linear system that has been with us since Socrates. Western man sees his system of logic as synonymous with the truth. For him it is the only road to reality."[43]

The classical way. A keystone of this familiar logic, typically ascribed to Aristotle, is the "Law of Identity: whatever is, is."[44] The reasoning is based upon the already mentioned "'Is' of identity" thinking. In other words, A *is* A in toto, anywhere, anytime, under any circumstances. Clearly, therefore, "A is not non-A." This statement is called the "Law of Contradiction."[45]

Another corollary of the Law of Identity, "A = A", is the Law of Sameness,[46] which may be expressed as: $A_1 = A_2 = A_3 ... = A_n$. When the idea of identity is applied to the same thing or person, the subscripts would correspond with different times, spaces, and contexts to indicate the thing or individual staying the same through all the vicissitudes. As unlikely as that sounds in actual life, many of us believe or yearn to believe in the permanence. We expect our magnificent creations (e.g., the Seven Wonders of the World) to withstand the elements forever. Similarly, we hope our friends to remain unchanged, eternally young, beautiful, and healthy —only, of course, to be chagrined to find, in class reunions and elsewhere, the inescapable ravages of time and tide.

On the other hand, the subscripts in the Sameness equation may correspond to individual things or persons in the same cluster of categorization. For instance, when traveling overseas, we often assume an invariance across cultures and feel inconvenienced by the unavailability of familiar commodities and services. Of course, even similarly packaged and identically labeled drugs, toiletries, soft drinks, or food items are simply not the same (try the ubiquitous hamburgers and pizzas as ready examples!). The variations in monetary units and the scales of measurement (length, weight, volume, size, etc.) add to our confusion and irritation.

Furthermore, we tend to get ourselves confounded by naively expecting the same services from similar workers. An example is the functions performed by realtors and lawyers in, say, the house purchasing process in the U.S. and U.K. While American realtors serve as a coordinator of, and an intermediary in, all aspects of transaction among the interested parties from beginning to end, British estate agents turn the whole business over to solicitors beyond the initial phases of property advertisement and the locating of a would-be buyer. Apparently, these two cultures, so close to each other, are divided by more than the "same" language!

In the same vein, where the people themselves, who are subsumed under the same category, are concerned, the tendency is for us to believe every member of the group to be identical to all others. As noted in Chapter 6, this presumption of uniformity can lead to much misunderstanding and social harm. Prejudice and discrimination feed off this Sameness principle.

The Law of Identity also gives rise to another trademark perspective of the Aristotelian way of reasoning, namely, its "two-valued, either-or orientation."[47] This dualistic perspective is abundantly revealed in "the stress on polarities, opposite ends of a scale, mutually exclusive opposites in Plato's sense."[48] Thus, students are presented with the dichotomous, yes-no choices on many of the so-called objective tests and, likewise, hesitant trial witnesses are sternly admonished by the judge, "Answer the question, Yes or No!" And, if someone is not *with* you, he or she must be *against* you. In the same manner, patriotism is often seen as a matter of loving the country or leaving it—"Our country, right or wrong!" or "If you don't like it here, go back to Africa (or Asia or wherever else)!" And there is another apposite declaration by a legendary football coach, Vince Lombardi: "Winning isn't everything. It's the *only* thing!" Indeed, even at such a superb level of athletic prowess, and in spite of the famous admonition of Count de Coubertin,[49] few Olympians are remembered and celebrated nowadays unless they managed to win a Gold medal (or, somewhat grudgingly, a Silver) in certain, choice sports disciplines. A Bronze medal or less amounts to little in fame or wealth in any discipline.

The critical significance of the conjunction, "or," in all such two-valued judgments was summed up in what Korzybski called the "Law of Excluded Middle: everything must either be *or* not be."[50] It follows that "A cannot be A *and* non-A, neither A *nor* non-A."[51] Choices are indeed few and clear-cut!

The trouble is that the two-valued logic "leaves out context" of experience,[52] and do not leave much room for conditional qualifications ("depending upon...") or situational interpretations ("under the particular circumstances..."). Technological applications may not miss this omission much,[53] but human meanings suffer from this decontextualization. In the American judiciary system, for example, "according to the opinion rule, only established facts, stripped of all contexting background data, are admissible as evidence.... The common inadmissibility of contexting testimony, including hearsay, sets our courts apart [from those in many other cultures] and frequently makes them harsh, inhuman, and impersonal."[54]

The same orientation is reflected in the one-thing-at-a-time, one-thing-after-another system of "monochronic time."[55] Typically in the cultures of Northern Europe and America, everything and everyone is (and must be) neatly scheduled and discretely processed on time and in time. The resultant operational efficiency is bought with time—which is, after all, money! In the contrasting, "many-things-at-a-time" system of "polychronic time," the simultaneous, multiple personal involvements are much more important, and communications are high-context in that most of "the meaning is in the context while very little is [explicitly] in the transmitted message." Accordingly, in the cultures of the latter category, more common in the Mediterranean region, native America, Latin America, the Middle East, and elsewhere, "schedules are handled quite differently; in fact, there are times when it is difficult to determine whether a schedule exists or not."[56]

In passing, it is worth noting that, even in the predominantly monochronic, low-context, two-valued Western cultures, the tasks traditionally undertaken by women tend to require a much more polychronic, high-context, multi-valued orientation than those assigned to men. This can be readily seen in the *simple* provision of meals wherein multiple preparatory and cooking activities must be coordinated so as to insure a synchronized culmination. A sequential, one-thing-at-a time handling of component tasks (e.g., the peeling of varied fruits, mixing of salad, cooking of vegetables, roasting of meats, brewing of drinks, heating of the serving dishes, setting of the table, ad infinitum) will be a sheer disaster—as, sadly, I personally know too well! By the time we speak of "mothering," the need for the capacity for varied parallel activities and deep yet flexible involvement becomes paramount. Many of us have watched almost in disbelief some mothers and babysitters who somehow manage to stay placid through the cacophony and maelstrom of young lives, sense all the goings-on as if with extra eyes and ears, relate to children individually and collectively, and calmly take care of multiple needs and crises without, in a manner of speaking, missing a beat. It goes without saying that the same admirable qualities are called for in nursing, care giving, and teaching, and other activities historically carried by more women than men.

Overall, meanwhile, a "lineal codification of reality" pervades the classical manner of reasoning. It proceeds "from parts to wholes, ... from isolated events to cause-and-effect sequences and changes." It has been acknowledged that this lineal perspective "with stress on discrete items undoubtedly has been a major factor in the development of Western science. But it may be that making other kinds of experience accessible to understanding, and further development of science itself, requires an expansion of this way of thought."[57] After all, "neither science nor rationality are [*sic*] universal measures of excellence. They are particular traditions, unaware of their historical grounding."[58]

Another way of reasoning. Even though the Aristotelian logic has been the dominant tradition, there are numerous other, legitimate ways to reason since, "ultimately, what makes sense (or not) is irrevocably culturally determined and depends heavily on the context in which the evaluation is made."[59] One of these differing traditions, typically identified with Georg Friedrich Hegel, seems to offer an interesting alternative to the classical orientation. In the Hegelian logic, the declaration, A *is* A, is not the last word. In fact, that is where the whole new story begins, because "the very comprehension of being requires a simultaneous grasp of nonbeing or absence.... All are distinguished by virtue of what they are not." Similarly, "Action proceeds and is only intelligible against the backdrop of its negation."[60] So, to understand fully what is true, moral, or beautiful requires a concurrent understanding of what is *not* true, moral, or beautiful. The decision to act one way is made in the knowledge, no matter how implicit or incomplete, of other ways, including the one of not-to-act.

"There is more in the world [beyond the Law of Identity]; there is an other. [Further,] this other, this more is in one sense an opposite, but it is an opposite continuous with and growing out of the original conception, not postulated as being at the opposite pole from it."[61] The thinking here is not dichotomous, discrete, and exclusive as in the Aristotelian logic of "A *is* A; thus, A is *not* non-A; hence, one can only be *either* A *or* non-A." Instead of the emphasis on the conjunction, "or," in the classical tradition, the Hegelian perspective stresses "and" and "also": everything and everybody is more than what we perceive; A is A, but A is *also* non-A. The general principle was captured in a statement by Chuang-tzu (or Zhuang-zi), an influential Tao philosopher of the 4th century, B.C.: "That which is one is one. That which is not-one, is also one."[62]

The contrast here leads to a large difference in the practical realm of life. I fondly remember a senior professor who left a strong impression on me in my salad days. To cover up my ignorance and insecurity, I was wont to take a particular stance in debates, vehemently trying to argue down any others. However, this mature colleague remained at ease throughout the discussion, treating dissenting interpretations with a sincere response: "You know, you *may be* right. Let's see where that one takes us. How would it handle this aspect? What about that aspect?" Soon I started noticing the constructive effects of the innocuous sounding, initial remark. It was not a "yes-no," "either-or" judgment. Though he had a very keen mind, he was not saying, "I am right, you are wrong," or its reverse. It was a simple acknowledgment of the actuality and legitimacy of multiple possibilities and, through that, a confirmation of each faculty as a person of worth. Later, some business friends of mine also found this orientation salutary in the cooperative work of their corporate teams.

In the same vein, the Hegelian manner of reasoning makes it easier for us to look at people as complex beings that they are. An individual is not single dimensional, just strong *or* weak, bright *or* dumb, good *or* bad. Instead, he or she is both, situating herself or himself on the multifaceted continua according to variable organismic and contextual factors. An upright church deacon may easily be a collector of *innocent* souvenir items purloined from hotels, restaurants, and even some shops, and a ruthless gangster and an unfaithful spouse can be a devoted parent. It is quite possible for a powerful, aggressive person to be simultaneously a superstitious one fearful of dark alleys and cemeteries. Quite a few quiet, modest-living spinsters and bachelors have posthumously caught others by surprise for being rich, generous benefactors of some good causes. While the Aristotelian reasoning tends to reduce people to size and sunders them, the Hegelian one allows people to take on their full dimensions, so to speak, and thereby accommodates both human nobilities and follies.

In the latter sense, "Man could contain more than himself.... The Renaissance thinkers were right when they said that man, the Microcosm, contains the Macrocosm."[63] The contrasts between some features of the two perspectives are schematized in Figure 7-2.

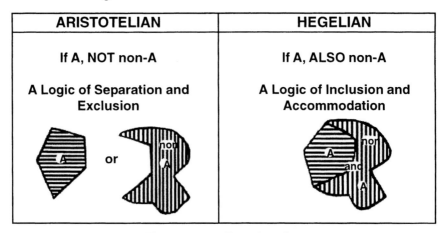

ARISTOTELIAN	**HEGELIAN**
If A, NOT non-A	If A, ALSO non-A
A Logic of Separation and Exclusion	A Logic of Inclusion and Accommodation

Figure 7-2. Two Logics

The Paradox of Life

It is likely that, puzzling over the preceding descriptions, many a reader said to himself or herself, "This does not make sense at all. The Hegelian logic is self-contradictory!" What needs to be kept in mind, however, is that "its 'logic' ... may well be 'illogical' when judged from the point of view of a particular system of formal logic,"[64] which is the Aristotelian one in this case. In other words, the consistency or inconsistency of a given way of reasoning must be judged *within* the particular system of logic. "Inasmuch as a person lives in a culture in which the correctness of Aristotelian logic is not doubted, it is exceedingly difficult, if not impossible, for him to be aware of experiences which contradict Aristotelian logic, hence which from the standpoint of his culture are nonsensical.... [Some] experience, which from the standpoint of paradoxical logic is quite 'logical,' does not make sense from the standpoint of Aristotelian logic."[65]

The notion of paradox. The Hegelian logic is also called "dialectical" or "paradoxical" logic to reflect the crucial significance of paradox in it. Although many seemingly absurd or self-contradictory statements are routinely clustered under the label of paradox, "paradoxes have generally been considered an embarrassment in the history of philosophy,"[66] since they cannot be easily handled by classical logic. A pronouncement like "All Cretans are liars," reputedly made by the Cretan prophet Epimenides, places philosophers in a quandary, since "if it were true, it would involve its own falsity."[67] The Aristotelian reasoning insists that a statement must be either true or false, not both.

However, what is at issue centrally in the non-traditional logic is "paradox [as] contradiction that inheres in the nature of things."[68] A couple of physical examples may clarify this recognized feature of inherence. In the field of topology, we come across a peculiar phenomenon of certain continuous surfaces with only one side, that is to say, without any distinction of the inside from the outside. The first such surface was discovered by, and named after, the mathematician August Moebius (1790-1868). If one traces the Moebius strip [see Figure 7-3] with a marker, starting on whichever side and never lifting it off the surface, she or he will be surprised to see that the drawn line appears on both sides of the strip. Thus there is actually *only* one side, not two. The strip may be formed by twisting a long ribbon of material 180 degrees and then joining the two ends. The three-dimensional version of such a surface was found later by another mathematician Felix Klein (1849-1925). The so-called Klein bottle is a long, tapered tube of which the smaller end loops back to penetrate the surface of the tube itself and then connects with the open, larger end [Figure 7-3]. Here also, the outside and the inside are one and the same.

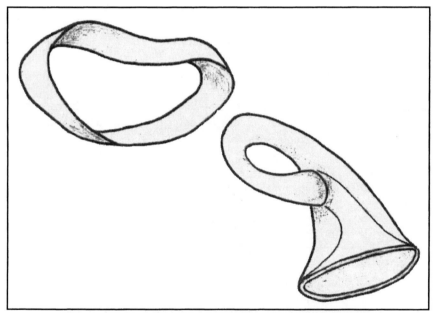

Figure 7-3. A Moebius Strip and a Kline Bottle

A paradox talked about more often is found in the field of physics wherein the nature of light was hotly debated around the turn of the 19th-20th centuries. The works of such physicists as Max Planck (1858-1947), Albert Einstein (1879-1955), Niels Bohr (1885-1962), Erwin Schrödinger (1887-1961), Louis de Broglie (1892-1987), Wolfgang Pauli (1900-1958), Werner Heisenberg (1901-1976), and Paul Dirac (1902-1984) led, not without some lively disagreements among them, to the development of quantum mechanics. Light is now understood as *both* corpuscular (a series of particles) *and* ondular (waves) in nature, not in terms of the "either-or." It is also acknowledged that what is being observed (e.g., atomic particles) is inescapably changed by the intervention of the observer and the instruments of observation (i.e., the extensions in use). The subjective thus affects the objective, and vice versa.

Another paradox more recently recognized is in the laser technology application to the lens-less photography. The technical details aside, what is remarkable is that, even when the resultant photographic plate is broken up into many pieces, each fragment retains a smaller, though fainter, image of the full hologram. That is to say, "Every part contains the whole.... [or] the wonder of the whole [is] revealed in every part." [69] This phenomenon of "the whole in every part" again goes against the common sense in the tradition of Aristotelian logic. Yet, it has been suggested by some neuroscientists that human brains operate as a holographic process to create the remarkable distributed memory.[70] Edward Hall speculates that this hologram quality may also explain the integrated character of cultures: "Cultures are integrated wholes, all of the parts interrelate and are reflected in each other."[71]

In the Hegelian way of reasoning, the contradiction of opposites is not seen as a "problem" requiring a resolution in some reconciliation "resulting from discovering some 'lowest common denominator.'... Hegel's syntheses ... do not do away with oppositions through compromise but preserve and transcend them (through the principle of *Aufhebung*) often in explicitly paradoxical form." Indeed, thesis and antithesis are an essential condition for rising to a higher level of "unity-in-distinction."[72] In other words, "dialectical contradiction is not a relation of static opposites but negativity, viz. active contradiction moving towards synthesis....The inherent nature ... of human experience... *is* to develop actively from level to level."[73] Thus contradiction and reconciliation together pervade every phase of the dialectic.

This notion of unity-in-distinction was illustrated in Elie Wiesel's comments on the occasion of Forum 2000 (Prague, September 3-7, 1997). Organized through the initiative of Czech president Vaclav Havel and Wiesel himself, this forum saw a large participation of world leaders in theology, philosophy, literature, arts, sciences, and politics to discuss an enlightenment into the new millenium. In response to an interviewer's question about the apparent opposition between the specificity of individual cultures and the uniformity through globalization, Wiesel observed: "The universality of the human message [paradoxically] rests in its specificity. [For instance,] no writer was more German than Goethe, more French than Victor Hugo, more English than Shakespeare, more Jewish than Jeremiah and Isaiah—yet, through their ethnic or national spirit, they succeed in pointing towards the universal.... Each culture expresses the thirst for transcending itself without denying what makes it unique."[74] His comments remind us of Hegel's own: "each individual consciousness raises itself out of its allotted sphere.... and therefore can only realize itself in a work which is a work of the whole."[75]

Upon noticing the seeming contradiction in paradox, we may mutter to ourselves, "This is ludicrous. It is nonsense." However, "what characterizes man is the richness and subtlety, the variety and versatility of his nature.... Rational thought, logical and metaphysical thought can comprehend only those objects which are free from contradiction, and which have a consistent nature and truth. It is, however, just this homogeneity we never find in man.... Contradiction is the very element of human existence."[76] Thus, being clearly aware of this human condition, Zen masters organize their "mon-dos" (questions and answers) and "ko-ans" (declarations for contemplation) around it. "Nonsensical though all this may be, it is only from our habit of conceptualization that we miss facing the ultimate reality as it stands nakedly by itself."[77] This same, desired process of liberation from the habitual perspective was described in a Western treatise as follows:

> The ordinary procedure ... of thought in common sense and science... Hegel calls the Understanding as opposed to the Reason.... Only the Reason possesses the complete truth, up to which the merely partial truth of the Understanding leads.... What the Understanding denies is the possibility of combining two contrary notions as they stand.... What the Reason does, is to merge these ideas in a higher one, in which their opposition, while in one sense preserved, is also transcended.... Reason is not contrary to, but beyond the Understanding.... For the distinctive mark of the Reason is, as Hegel says, that "it apprehends the unity of the categories in their opposition."[78]

Indeed, it was Hegel's opinion that, "To see that thought in its very nature is dialectical, and that, as understanding, it must fall into contradiction,—the negative of itself, will form one of the main lesson of logic."[79]

Transcendence. Meanwhile, reflecting upon a well-known Greek myth, Albert Camus offers an illustration of the transcendental reasoning. Sisyphus, the former king of Corinth, once betrayed a secret of Zeus who, in his wrath, condemned Sisyphus to Hades. There, he was to roll a heavy rock eternally up a mountain. Of course, every time he almost pushed it to the top, the rock would escape his grasp and tumble down to the valley bottom. In Zeus's view, such a useless and hopeless task would be the severest possible punishment for his misdeeds. As a result, for countless times a day, Sisyphus had to toil up the hill, then climb down after the fallen rock for yet another try.

However, Camus sees this pause for descent as a critical time for contemplation. Of course, Sisyphus is fully conscious of the enormity of his misfortune, but he is also clearly aware of his paradoxical freedom. In every step down, he is sustained by the hope for success the next time. He reviews the past attempts and formulates a new plan for action. He has a project for his life, and he is stronger than the rock. In other words, he is above his fate, and the final say shall be his. In spite of the harsh trials and tribulations, he can judge that all is well, thereby achieving his paradoxical triumph through transcendence. Accordingly, Camus concludes that Sisyphus must be imagined happy.[80]

"The sense of life … is nothing other than each one's acceptance of his inexorable circumstance and, on accepting it, converting it into his own creation."[81] Thus, "man makes himself in the light of circumstance, and he is a God as occasion offers, a 'secondhand God'…."[82] "Finally, therefore, everything depends on the attitude of the particular individual to the given factors, including primarily himself."[83]

Obviously, the re-creation as a "secondhand god" demands an awareness and the courage to be, which is "self-affirmation 'in spite of'."[84] Such self-affirmation also requires receptivity, acceptance, and fortitude, transcending the typical dichotomy of activity vs. passivity, mobility vs. stability, firmness vs. flexibility, and the like. Nietzsche couches the challenge as follows:

> Do you have courage, O my brothers?
> Are you brave?…. Brave is he who knows fear but *conquers* fear, who sees the abyss, but with *pride*; who grasps the abyss with the talons of an eagle—that man has courage.[85]

In every walk. Over the centuries, transcendence has often been revealed in the crucible of human tragedy. Some of the tenderest, bravest, and noblest deeds, thoughts, and sentiments have found their expressions under some horrific conditions of life and death, for example, in the times of war, disaster, and pestilence. Some of the episodes are widely known—in the 1912 sinking of the Titanic, in and around the Nazi death camps during the Second World War, and in the September 2001 terrorist attacks on the New York World Trade Center and the Pentagon, and so on. However, the experience does not have to be so dramatic, and many people have attained the paradoxical synthesis with dignity in their quiet, everyday living and dying. Only several, random samples need be mentioned here.

A seven-year-old Ben Oyler was stricken with AIDS through faulty blood transfusion and died two years later. In spite of his young age, he had come to show remarkable awareness and acceptance of his condition. Two days before his death, he was preparing a will with the help of his mother. Here is the mother's record.

> Tears began falling on Ben's journal as I was writing. And Grant [the father] brushed his own tears away with his arm, hoping Ben wouldn't notice. We couldn't help it, just listening to Ben give away the things that had mattered so much to him. "I—don't—want you guys to be sad—okay?" His voice was deep and hoarse. Grant and I looked at each other. This wasn't the way we wanted Ben to see us…. "Okay, Ben," I said. "It's just that we'll miss you a lot, that's all." "I'll miss you too," he said.[86]

Arnold Beisser, whom we already met in Chapter 4 (Footnote 34) and Chapter 5 (Footnote 10), had to spend three years confined in an iron lung, totally dependent upon others for his own survival. He recounts:

> When I stopped trying to figure out how to get out of my predicament, and got involved with it instead, I discovered that the unpleasant and disagreeable aspects changed. As I allowed myself to be fully where and who I was in this moment, without planning for the next—this moment, this place, and I myself changed.... To be here and to sense the wonder, the awe, the horror, the tragedy, the comedy, is the privilege of life.... There is only this alone. It is enough.[87]

In the meantime, a home-maker and journalist, Linda Weltner, described the path of her development this way.

> I wanted to create a home full of love and acceptance for my family, but first, I had to learn to love and accept myself.... Though I became a newspaper reporter when our youngest daughter was three, making a home for my husband and children became my life's work. It was a task that claimed me and energized me and transformed me from a troubled young girl into a woman capable of taking responsibility for her life. In the process I fashioned myself a home. What I dreamed for others, I attained for myself.[88]

Finally, in a book she published at the age of 85, Florida Scott-Maxwell gave a cogent summary to life's paradox in the following words. She was a home-maker and writer, but also a psychoanalyst who had started her training with Carl Jung himself when she was 50.

> I often want to say to people, "You have neat, tight expectations of what life ought to give you, but you won't get it. That isn't what life does. Life does not accommodate you, it shatters you. It is meant to, and it couldn't do it better. Every seed destroys its container or else there would be no fruition."[89]

The self and the other. Meanwhile, the required awareness for transcendence has its own paradox, which Hegel explicated in his example of the relationship between Master (the lord) and Slave (the bondsman). As paraphrased by Kainz:

> The opposition ... is transcended ... at that moment when there is a reciprocal recognition on the part of both Master and Slave of the paradoxical facts that the Master's dependence on the Slave is a form of slavery, and that the Slave's dominance over the objective world through his work makes him a free and independent self-consciousness, a Master.[90]

"It is clear that being-*in-itself* and being-*for-an-other* are one and the same [since] action by one side only would be useless because what is to happen can only be brought about by both.... [when] they *recognize* themselves as *mutually recognizing* one another."[91] The same paradox was poetically described by Rebecca West as follows:

> Surely in each human being there is both a hungry naked outcast and a Sister of Charity, desolate without those whom she can feed and clothe and shelter, and these cannot minister to each other. That is the rule which has been put in to make it more difficult. They must find a stranger outside the skin to whose Sister of Charity the outcast can offer his rose, to whose outcast the Sister of Charity can offer her pity.[92]

This "rule" has been well noted by others, especially those who try to serve as a catalyst for human development. For instance, Viktor Frankl observed that one becomes truly human, "not by concerning himself with his self's actualization, but by forgetting himself and giving himself, overlooking himself and focusing outward."[93] Similarly, Floyd Matson pointed out the vital connection, fully understood by Otto Rank, "between independence and *inter*-dependence — the fact that human person is brought to maturity not through alienation but through affiliation. 'The ego needs the other,' at each successive stage of self-development, in order to be confirmed in the recognition of its own identity."[94]

Life is a gift, but it is also a task. "At the moment of birth, life asks man a question, and this question he must answer. He must answer it at every moment; not his mind, not his body, but *he ... the whole man ...* must answer it.... The question is: ... how can we find union within ourselves, with our fellowman, with nature? ... This is a question by the very fact of his existence ... a question raised by the contradiction within himself—that of being in nature and at the same time of transcending nature by the fact that he is life aware of itself."[95]

Young or old, therefore, a person must wrestle with the fundamental question in various guises, and strive for transcendence of the essential paradox with awareness, fortitude, and courage. That is the lifetime challenge and the opportunity for all of us.

Notes

1. Hall, 1983, 209.
2. Hall, 1977.
3. Hall, 1983, 209.
4. It should be recalled that, where people drive on the left, the steering wheel is on the right side of the vehicle. Thus, when making a left turn, the driver is farther away than the front seat passenger from a pedestrian who is stepping into the crosswalk parallel to the original direction of the car's travel. Sharply looking back to the right, the alarmed pedestrian thus sees the one in the passenger seat first.
5. W. Johnson and Moeller, 1972, 172.
6. Heath and Tindale, 1994, 1.
7. Lurigio, Carroll, and Stalans, 1994, 106, 107, 108.
8. Heath, Tindale, Edwards et al., 1994.
9. Schwartz, 1994, 68-69.
10. Hall, 1977, 123.
11. "Amelia Bedelia" is the main character in a series of humorous books by Peggy Parish. "Asterix" and "Obelix" are two of the Gallic warriors battling the Roman Legions in the *Asterix* cartoon series, created by René Goscinny and Albert Uderzo. "Sergent Snorkel," "Private Zero," and "Private Beetle Bailey" are among the main characters of Mort Walker's cartoon series, *Beetle Bailey.*
12. Hayakawa, 1964, 189.
13. Polanyi, 1962, vii, 57.
14. Korzybski, 1948, 165.
15. Hall, 1977, 144.
16. Korzybski, 1948, 417.
17. Ibid., 35.
18. Aichhorn, 1936.
19. Black, 1962, 228.
20. R. Brown, 1989, 84.
21. Korzybski, 1948, 375.
22. Yamamoto, 1975, 86.
23. Lynd, 1961, 114.
24. Ibid., 76-77.
25. Max Picard, quoted in Eiseley, 1980, 137.
26. Yamamoto, 1975, 81.
27. Polanyi, 1967, 19, 18.
28. Ibid., 36.
29. LeVine, 1984, 80.
30. Lynd, 1961, 115.
31. Ibid., 117.

32. From my teaching experiences at several American universities, I may be tempted to characterize this oversight *willing*. One of the predictable questions raised by doctoral students is, "How far back must I go in the literature review for my dissertation?" The common advice, at least in human and social sciences, appears to be, "Go back a decade or two, five at most." In the *throw-away, planned obsolescence* culture of America, the new is obviously king while the old is a useless curse, even including most classics in the very disciplines of study. Many students, raised on the diet of digest textbooks and internet downloads, seem to welcome the already interpreted and organized, instantly available, and *up-to-date* materials, shunning the slow, laborious deciphering on their own of the ancient *gibberish and rubbish!* In this connection, one is reminded of Gunnar Myrdal's trenchant observation: "Ignorance — like knowledge — is seldom random but is instead highly opportunistic" (1969, 99).

33. Ortega y Gasset, 1962, 217.

34. Bronowski, 1981, 14. Though he speaks only of scientist in this quotation, Bronowski's comments seem equally apt when applied to artist. For instance, the diversity and technical complexity of the so-called primitive art of the stone age, which is at least 20,000 years old and more recently discovered in, among other places, the Ardèche valley of France, have strongly suggested that the tempting supposition of "the most original achievement of the mind" being "also the most recent" would not necessarily hold in the artistic realm, either [see, e.g., Gély, 2000]. In yet another realm of life, note also that the very complete fossil skeleton of a newborn , known as "Le Moustier 2," has revealed that the Neanderthals were already practicing intentional burial 40,000 years ago [see, e.g., Maureille, 2002].

35. Feyerabend, 1993, 35, 33.

36. Hoffer, 1958, preface, i, 82, 80-81.

37. Ibid., 24.

38. Rokeach, 1960, 225.

39. Hoffer, 1958, 25.

40. Hall, 1977, 220.

41. Fromm, 1974, 102, 99, 100.

42. Ibid., 101.

43. Hall, 1977, 9.

44. Korzybski, 1948, 404.

45. Fromm, 1974, 101.

46. W. Johnson, 1946.

47. Korzybski, 1948.

48. Lynd, 1961, 82.

49. Barron Pierre de Coubertin (1863-1937) was a French educator who renovated the Olympic Games. Like the classic, Panhellenic ones, the

modern, international version takes place every four years since 1896 (Athens) and 1900 (Paris). In his famous speech, Coubertin, 1908, argued: "The important thing in life is not the victory but the contest; the essential thing is not to have won but to have fought well." (Cook, 1909).

50. Korzybski, 1948, 404.
51. Fromm, 1974, 101.
52. Hall, 1983, 132. Also see, Hall, 1989.
53. Quite symbolic here is the remarkable development of the semiconductor technology. The relays in microchip circuits, which are the heart of electronic machines like modern computers, work on the binary logic of "go *or* no go." Some analysts (e.g., Burke and Ornstein, 1995) appear to continue to pin their hopes on even newer technological prowess for solving world problems.
54. Hall, 1977, 107.
55. Hall, 1977, 1983; Hall and Hall, 1989.
56. Hall, 1983, 210, 211.
57. Lynd, 1961, 80, 81.
58. Feyerabend, 1993, 214. Myrdal's observations [1969, 9] are also relevant here: "Facts do not organize themselves into concepts and theories just by being looked at; indeed, except within the framework of concepts and theories, there are no scientific facts but only chaos. There is an inescapable *a priori* element in all scientific work. Questions must be asked before answers can be given. The questions ... are at bottom valuations. Valuations are thus necessarily involved already at the stage when we observe facts and carry on theoretical analysis...."
59. Hall, 1977, 214.
60. Gergen, 1997, 9.
61. Lynd, 1961, 134.
62. Fromm, 1974, 102. In the same vein, the Chinese perspective does not dichotomize the good and the evil, but consider both to be the integral parts of the process of life itself. (See, e.g., Gernet, 2005; Jullien 2004.) The rejection of the dualism has also been the basic tenet of Zen Buddhism. (See, e.g., Suzuki, 1961.)
63. Eiseley, 1980, 176.
64. Feyerabend, 1993, 191.
65. Fromm, 1974, 102. The difficulty noted by Fromm directly leads to the experience characterized by Menard as follows: [T]hinking dialectically is something that American intellectuals don't naturally do. John Dewey was one of the few who did, and Dewey was trained as a Hegelian. American critics tend to prefer a binary analysis: thumbs up or thumbs down, right or left, tonic or toxin. It is difficult for them to see that most cultural products work in several ways at once. It is even harder for them to see that each element in a cultural system depends for its

value on all others—so that to alter one element is to alter every element. Their overpowering impulse is ... to isolate and to simplify" (2003, 82).

66. Kainz, 1988, 1.
67. Korzybski, 1948, 739.
68. Lynd, 1961, 254. [For a discussion of the inherent spatial paradox in the Klein bottle and the like, see, e.g., Rucker, 1977.]
69. Trevelyan, 1990. This intersting feature of the hologram (i.e., even when broken, each part still reproduces the whole image) is due to the fact that no lens is used to form image and, hence, "each point on the hologram has received light from all parts of the object" (Hariharan, 1991, 513). Thus, "a fragment of the hologram is like a small window," and "the observer can see just as much through the small window" (Leith, 1995, 305).
70. Harth, 1982; Pribram, 1971.
71. Hall, 1989, 31. Also see, Reinsmith, 1989.
72. Kainz, 1988, 32, 36.
73. Mure, 1950, 302, 355.
74. Wiesel, 1997, 28.
75. Hegel, 1977, 357.
76. Cassirer, 1944, 11.
77. Suzuki, 1974, 45.
78. McTaggert, 1922, 14-15, 89, 88.
79. Wallace, 1959, 18-19.
80. Camus, 1942, 161-165.
81. José Ortega y Gasset, quoted in May, 1981, 93.
82. Ortega y Gasset, 1962, 206.
83. Rank, 1978, 206.
84. Tillich, 1952, 150.
85. Kaufmann, 1976, 400.
86. Oyler, 1988, 229.
87. Beisser, 1990b , 170.
88. Weltner, 1990, xiii.
89. Scott-Maxwell, 1979, 65.
90. Kainz, 1988, 36.
91. Hegel, 1977, 104, 112.
92. Rebecca West, quoted in Sarton, 1973, 202.
93. Frankl, 1978, 35.
94. Matson, 1966, 206.
95. Fromm, 1974, 87, 92.

Epilogue

In this brief treatise, we examined our cultural extensions, namely, the devices of human creation with which the species continues its evolution. Whether more material (physical) or nonmaterial (mental), more concrete or abstract, they have helped us to extend our organismic functions by amplifying our power and augmenting our control over the environment, ourselves, and other people. They have been an essential part of our life since Day Six of Creation. Indeed, these extensions are omnipresent in human life, and they have proven indispensable for many purposes in varied contexts.

However, as we have seen, they are definitely double-edged means, and their ready availability and very power itself can prove destructive when used by the unaware or the malevolent. To reiterate Paul Tillich's apt observation here;

> The man-created world of objects has drawn into itself him who created it and who now loses his subjectivity in it. He has sacrificed himself to his own productions.... Man, for whom all this was invented as a means, becomes a means himself in the service of means.[1]

It goes without saying that "all these magnified human powers are the result of human desires, human contrivances, human efforts."[2] Everything begins and ends with the mediation of the unique organism that we are. This is the reason why the more abstract extensions deserve even closer attention than that directed at the more concrete, tangible varieties. Undeniably, much truth is to be found in the saying that there is nothing more powerful than ideas, *mere* ideas!

The question is how to develop and utilize the full potential of extensions for the good of all without being hamstrung or destroyed by their very power and scope. They could be harnessed so as to recognize and enhance what Loren Eiseley called the "faint light ... [that] entered into [our] nature a curious wistful gentleness and courage.... [With that inner light,] man, the animal, sought to be something that no animal had been before.... For man may grow until he towers to the sky, but without this light he is nothing, and his place is nothing."[3]

The task is to utilize extensions judiciously in cultivating our sensibilities, tenderness, sincerity, thoughtfulness, imaginativeness, and fortitude, while curtailing our greed, vanity, ignorance, callousness, bigotry, belligerence, and cruelty. Simultaneously, the same task obliges us to prevent the very force and reach of extensions to work in our face, augmenting the evil and diminishing the good. For a successful campaign, the 2,500-year-old wisdom in *Sun-Tsu* dictates that one know well both one's own army, i.e., ourselves, and the opposing army, which is the oft-ignored features of cultural extensions. The efforts are not easy but certainly worthwhile since, in the inimitable words of Saint-Exupéry,

> While it is good that various things [*read*, extensions] were to be created to serve humans, it would be monstrous if humans themselves were to serve as the dump for such things."[4]

Notes

1. Tillich, 1952, 139, 138.
2. Mumford, 1952, 16.
3. Eiseley, 1980, 145-146.
4. Saint-Exupéry, 1948, 231.

References

Adorno, Theodor W., Frenkel-Brunswick, Elyse, Levinson, Daniel J., and Sanford, R. Nevitt. 1950. *The Authoritarian Personality*. New York: Harper.

Aichhorn, August. 1936. *The Wayward Youth*. London: Putnam.

Albom, Mitch. 1997. *Tuesdays with Morrie*. New York: Doubleday.

Allman, William F. 1994. *The Stone Age Present*. New York: Simon & Schuster.

Allport, Gordon W. 1937. *Personality*. New York: Holt.

_____. 1958. *The Nature of Prejudice*. Garden City, NY: Doubleday.

_____. 1961. *Pattern and Growth in Personality*. New York: Holt, Rinehart & Winston.

_____. 1964. *Personality and Social Encounter*. Boston: Beacon Press.

Axline, Virginia. 1964. *Dibs in Search of Self*. New York: Ballantine Books.

Bailey, George. 1974. *Germans*. New York: Avon Books.

Baker, Robert A. 1996. *Hidden Memories*. New York: Prometheus Books.

Barzini, Luigi. 1984. *Europeans*. New York: Penguin Books.

Bateson, Gregory. 1972. *Steps to an Ecology of Mind*. San Francisco: Chandler Publishing.

Baumeister, Roy F., ed. 1993. *Self-Esteem: The Puzzle of Low Self-Regard*. New York: Plenum.

Beauvilain, Alain, and Le Guellec, Yves. 2004. "Further Details concerning Fossils Attributed to *Sahelanthropus tchadensis* (Toumaï): Research in Action." *South African Journal of Science* 100 (3 & 4): 142-144.

Becker, Gay. 1999. *Disrupted Lives*. Berkeley, CA: University of California Press.

Becker, Howard S. 1966. *Outsiders*. New York: Free Press.

Beisser, Arnold. 1990a. *A Grateful Passage*. New York: Doubleday.

_____. 1990b. *Flying without Wings*. New York: Bantam Books.

Benedict, Ruth F. 1946. *The Chrysanthemum and the Sword*. Boston: Houghton Mifflin.

Bergson, Henri. 1975. *An Introduction to Metaphysics: The Creative Mind*. Totowa, NJ: Littlefield, Adams.

Berne, Eric. 1975. *Transactional Analysis in Psychotherapy*. New York: Ballantine Books.

Berque, Augustin. 1993. *Du Geste à la Cité*. Paris: Editions Gallimard.

_____. 1994. "Identification of the Self in Relation to the Environment." In *Japanese Sense of Self*, ed. Nancy Rosenberger, 93-104. Cambridge, U.K.: Cambridge University Press.

Black, Max. 1962. *Models and Metaphors*. Ithaca, NY: Cornell University Press.

Brim, Gilbert. 1992. *Ambition*. New York: Basic Books.

Bronowski, Jacob. 1978. *The Visionary Eye*. Cambridge, MA: The MIT Press.

_____. 1981. *The Ascent of Man*. London: Macdonald.

Brown, P., Sutikna, T., Morwood, M. J., Soejono, et al. 2004. "A New Small-Bodied Hominin from the Late Pleistocene of Flores, Indonesia." *Nature* 431 (October 28): 1055-1061.

Brown, Richard H. 1989. *A Poetic for Sociology*. Chicago: University of Chicago Press.

Bruner, Jerome S. 1962a. *On Knowing*. Cambridge, MA: Harvard University Press.

_____. 1962b. "The Conditions of Creativity." In *Contemporary Approaches to Creative Thinking,* eds. Howard E. Gruber, Glenn Terrell, and Michael Wertheimer, 1-30. New York: Atherton Press.

_____. 1966. *Toward a Theory of Instruction*. Cambridge, MA: Harvard University Press. .

_____. 1987. "Life as Narrative." *Social Research* 54: 11-32.

Brunet, Michel, Guy, Franck, et al. 2002. "A New Hominid from the Upper Miocene of Chad, Central Africa." *Nature* 418 (July 11): 145-151.

_____. 2005. "New Material of the Earliest Hominid from the Upper Miocene of Chad." *Nature* 434 (April 7): 752-755.

Buber, Martin. 1965. *Between Man and Man*. New York: Macmillan.

Burke, James, and Ornstein, Robert. 1995. *The Axmaker's Gift*. New York: G. P. Putnam's Sons.

Burns, Robert. 1968. "To a Mouse." In *The Poems and Songs of Robert Burns*, 3 vols., ed. James Kinsley. Oxford, U.K.: Clarendon. [Originally in *Poems Chiefly in the Scottish Dialect*, 1786, Kilmarnock, Scotland.]

Bushman, Brad J., and Baumeister, Roy F. 1998. "Threatened Egoism, Narcissism, Self-Esteem, and Direct and Misplaced Aggression: Does Self-Love or Self-Hate Lead to Violence? *Journal of Personality and Social Psychology* 75 (1): 219-229.

Camus, Albert. 1942. *Le Mythe de Sisyphe*. Paris: Editions Gallimard.

Canadian Broadcasting Corporation. 1983. "War," transcript of Program 2, "Anybody's Son Will Do." Kent, OH: PTV Publications.

Cassirer, Ernst. 1944. *An Essay on Man*. New Haven, CT: Yale University Press.

Chambers, Robert. 1981. "Education for Perspective — A Proposal." *Change* 13 (September): 48.

Chorlton, Windsor, et al. 1983. *Ice Ages*. Alexandria, VA: Time-Life Books.

Clausen, John A . 1995. *American Lives: Looking Back at the Children of the Great Depression*. Berkeley, CA: University of California Press.

Comer, James P. 1988. *Maggie's American Dream.* New York: New American Library.

Cook, T. A. 1909. *Fourth Olympiad.* London: British Olympic Association. [This was the official report on the 1908 Olympic Games in London.]

Cooley, Charles Horton. 1902. *Human Nature and the Social Order.* New York: Charles Scribner's Sons.

Cottle, Thomas. 1980. *Children's Secrets.* New York: Anchor Press/Doubleday.

Coubertin, Pierre de. 1908, July 24. Speech at a government banquet in London. [Recorded in T. A. Cook, *Fourth Olympiad* (London: British Olympic Association 1909).]

Cowley, Malcolm. 1982. *The View from 80.* New York: Penguin Books.

Cremin, Lawrence A. 1964. *Transformation of the Schools.* New York; McGraw-Hill.

Csordas, Thomas. 1990. "Embodiment as a Paradigm for Anthropology." *Ethos* 18: 5-47.

Darwin, Charles. 1859. *The Origin of Species.* London: John Murray.

_____. 1871. *The Descent of Man.* London: John Murray.

Doctorow, E. L. 1985. "The Passion of Our Calling." *The New York Times Book Review* (August 25): 1+.

Douglas, Mary, and Ney, Steven. 1998. *Missing Persons.* Berkeley, CA: University of California Press.

Drucker, Peter F. 1969. *The Age of Discontinuity.* New York: Harper and Row.

Dubos, René. 1968. *So Human an Animal.* New York: Charles Scribner's Sons.

_____. 1982. *Celebrations of Life.* New York: McGraw-Hill.

Dunne, John S. 1975. *Time and Myth.* Notre Dame, IN: University of Notre Dame Press.

Edelman, Marian Wright. 1992 *The Measure of Our Success.* Boston: Beacon Press.

Eiseley, Loren C. 1957. *The Immense Journey.* New York: Vintage Books.

_____. 1969. *The Unexpected Universe.* New York: Harcourt Brace Jovanovich.

_____. 1980. *The Firmament of Time.* New York: Atheneum.

Elkind, David. 1981. *The Hurried Child.* Reading, MA: Addison-Wesley.

Emler, Nicholas. 2001. *Self-Esteem: The Costs and Causes of Low Self-Worth.* [A report of the Joseph Rowntree Foundation, U.K.] York, England: York Publishing Services (64 Hallfield Road, Layerthorpe York YO31 7ZQ).

EPICA Community Members. 2004 (June 10). "Eight Glacial Cycles from an Antarctic Ice Core." *Nature* 429: 623-628.

Erikson, Erik H. 1974. *Dimensions of a New Identity.* New York: W. W. Norton.

_____. 1977. *Toys and Reasons.* New York: W. W. Norton

Erikson, Erik H., Erikson, Joan M., and Kivnick, Helen Q. 1986. *Vital Involvement in Old Age.* New York: W. W. Norton.

Eskin, Blake. 2002. *A Life in Pieces.* New York: W. W. Norton.

Eyer, Diane E. 1992. *Mother-Infant Bonding* New Haven, CT: Yale University Press.

Feyerabend, Paul. 1993. *Against Method*, 3rd ed. London: Verso.

Frankl, Viktor. 1978. *The Unheard Cry for Meaning*. New York: Simon and Schuster.

Friedenberg, Edgar. 1962. *The Vanishing Adolescent*. New York: Dell.

Friedman, Maurice. 1974. *The Hidden Human Image*. New York: Dell.

Fromm, Erich. 1965. *Escape from Freedom*. New York: Avon Books.

_____. 1967. *Man for Himself*. New York: Fawcett Books.

_____. 1971. *The Heart of Man*. New York: Harper and Row.

_____. 1974. "Psychoanalysis and Zen Buddhism." In *Zen Buddhism and Psychoanalysis,* by Erich Fromm, D. T. Suzuki, and Richard De Martino, 77-141. London: Souvenir Press.

Furet, François. 1994 "Le Destin d'une Idée." *France-Amérique* (San Francisco, July 9-15), R-T.

Gardner, John. 1987. *Excellence*, rev. ed. New York: W. W. Norton.

Gates, Henry L., Jr. 1994. *Colored People*. New York: Alfred A. Knopf.

Gaylin, Willard. 1991. *On Being and Becoming Human*. London: Penguin Books.

Gazzaniga, Michael S. 1998. *The Mind's Past*. Berkeley, CA: University of California Press.

Gearin-Tosh, Michael. 2002. *Living Proof: A Medical Mutiny*. New York: Charles Scribner's Sons.

Gély, Bernard. 2000. *Grottes Ornées de l'Ardèche*. Veurey, France: Éditions Le Dauphiné Libéré.

Gergen, Kenneth J. 1991. *The Saturated Self*. New York: Basic Books.

_____. 1997. *Realities and Relationships*. Cambridge, MA: Harvard University Press.

Gernet, Jacques. 2005. *La Raison des Choses: Essai sur la Philosophie de Wang Fuzhi (1619-1692)*. Paris : Gallimard.

Gibran, Kahlil. 1963. *The Prophet*. New York: Alfred A. Knopf.

Gilman, Dorothy. 1989. *A New Kind of Country*. New York: Fawcett, Ballantine.

Goffman, Erving. 1963. *Stigma*. Englewood Cliffs, NJ: Prentice-Hall.

Goodman, Mary Ellen. 1964. *Race Awareness in Young Children*, rev. ed. New York: Collier Books.

Gore, Rick. 2002. "The First Pioneer?" *National Geographic* 202 (August): no pagination.

Gorer, Geoffrey E. 1948. *The American People*. New York: W. W. Norton.

_____. 1955. *Exploring English Character*. New York: Criterion Books.

Gorer, Geoffrey E. 1962. "Introduction – 1961." In *The People of Great Russia* by Geoffrey Gorer and John Rickman, xxix-xli. New York: W. W. Norton.

Gorer, Geoffrey E. 1967. "English Character in the Twentieth Century." *The Annals of the American Academy of Political and Social Science* 370 (March): 74-81.

Gorer, Geoffrey E, and Rickman, John. 1949. *The People of Great Russia.* London: Cresset Press.

Gourevitch, Philip. 1999. "The Memory Thief." *The New Yorker* (June 14), 48-68.

Grumbach, Doris. 1995. *Extra Innings.* New York: W. W. Norton.

Guillemin, Victor. 1968. *The Story of Quantum Mechanics.* New York: Charles Scribner's Sons.

Hall, Edward T. 1969. *The Hidden Dimension.* Garden City, NY: Anchor Books.

_____. 1977. *Beyond Culture.* Garden City, NY: Anchor Books.

_____. 1983. *The Dance of Life.* Garden City, NY: Anchor Press/ Doubleday.

_____. 1989. "Unstated Features of the Cultural Context of Learning." *The Educational Forum* 54 (Fall): 21-34.

Hall, Edward T., and Hall, Mildred. 1989. *Understanding Cultural Differences: Germans, French, and Americans.* Yarmouth, Maine: Intercultural Press.

Hariharan, P. 1991. "Holography." In *The Encyclopedia of Physics,* 2nd ed., 512-516. New York: VCH Publishers.

Harth, Eric. 1982. *Windows on the Mind.* New York: William Morrow.

Hayakawa, S. I. 1964. *Language in Thought and Action,* 2nd ed. New York: Harcourt, Brace and World.

Heath, Linda, and Tindale, R. Scott. 1994. "Heuristics and Biases in Applied Settings: An Introduction." In *Applications of Heuristics and Biases to Social Issues,* eds. Linda Heath, R. Scott Tindale, John Edwards, et al., 1-12. New York: Plenum Press.

Heath, Linda, Tindale, R. Scott, Edwards, John, Posavac, Emil J., Bryant, Fred B., Henderson-King, Eaaron, Suarez-Balcazar, Yolanda, and Myers, Judith, eds. 1994. *Appilcations of Heuristics and Biases to Social Issues.* New York: Plenum Press.

Hegel, G. W. F. [1807] 1977. *Phenomenology of Spirit.* Oxford, U. K.: Oxford University Press.

Heisenberg, Werner. 1958. *Physics and Philosophy.* New York: Harper & Row.

Henle, Mary. 1962. "The Birth and Death of Ideas." In *Contemporary Approaches to Creative Thinking,* eds. Howard E. Gruber, Glenn Terrell, and Michael Wertheimer, 31-62. New York: Atherton Press.

Herbert, Martin. 1983. *Maternal Bonding.* Oxford, U.K.: Basil Blackwell.

Hirsch, Werner Z. 1964. "Administrative and Fiscal Considerations in Urban Development." *The Annals of the American Academy of Political and Social Science* 352 (March): 48-61.

Hoffer, Eric. 1958. *The True Believer*. New York: New American Library.
_____. 1964. *The Ordeal of Change*. New York: Harper and Row.
Horney, Karen. 1966. *Our Inner Conflict*. New York: W. W. Norton.
Hoyle, Fred. 1981. *Ice: The Ultimate Human Catastrophe*. New York: Continuum.
Huxley, Aldous. 1932. *Texts and Pretexts*. London: Chartto and Windus.
Imbrie, John, and Imbrie, Katherine Palmer. 1979. *Ice Ages*. Short Hills, NJ: Enslow Publishers.
Inkeles, Alex. 1997. *National Chraracter*. New Brunswick, NJ: Transaction Publishers.
Jackson, Mick. 1997. *The Underground Man*. New York: Penguin Books.
Johnson, Wendell. 1946. *People in Quandaries*. New York: Harper.
Johnson, Wendell, and Moeller, Dorothy. 1972. *Living with Changes*. New York: Harper and Row.
Jullien, François. 2004. *L'Ombre au Tableau: Du Mal ou du Negatif*. Paris: Seuil.
Kainz, Howard P. 1988. *Paradox, Dialectic, and System*. University Park, PA: Pennsylvania State University Press.
Kammen, Michael. 1997. "Some Patterns and Meanings of Memory Distortion in American History." In *Memory Distortion*, ed. Daniel L. Schacter, 329-345. Cambridge, MA: Harvard University Press.
Kaufman, Sharon R. 1986. *The Ageless Self*. Madison, WI: University of Wisconsin Press.
Kaufmann, Walter, ed. 1976. *The Portable Nietzsche*. Hammondsworth, Middlesex, England: Penguin Books.
Kingdon, Jonathan. 1993. *Self-made Man*. New York: John Wiley and Sons.
Klaus, Marshall H., Jerauld, Richard, Kreger, Nancy, McAlpine, Willie, Steffa, Meredith, and Kennell, John H. 1972. "Maternal Attachment: Importance of the First Postpartum Days." *New England Journal of Medicine* 286 (March): 460-463.
Klaus, Marshall H., and Kennell, John H. 1976 *Maternal-Infant Bonding*. St. Louis: Mosby.
Kohn, Alex. 1993. *Punished by Rewards: The Trouble with Gold Stars, Incentive Plans, A's, Praise, and Other Bribes*. Boston: Houghton Mifflin.
Koller, Alice. 1983. *An Unknown Woman*. New York: Bantam.
Korzybski, Alfred. 1948. *Science and Society*, 3rd ed. Lakeville, CT: The International Non-Aristotelian Library Publishing Co.
Kuhn, Thomas S. 1962. *The Structure of Scientific Revolutions*. Chicago: University of Chicago Press.
Kurland, Geoffrey. 2002. *My Own Medicine*. New York: Henry Holt..
Laban, Rudolf. 1974. *The Language of Movement*. Boston: Plays, Inc.
Labaree, David F. 1997. *How to Succeed in School Without Really Learning*. New Haven, CT: Yale University Press.

LaBarre, Weston. 1954. *The Human Animal.* Chicago: University of Chicago Press.

Lakoff, George, and Johnson, Mark. 1980. *Metaphors We Live By.* Chicago: University of Chicago Press.

_____. *Philosophy in the Flesh.* 1999. New York: Basic Books.

Lamb, Michael E. 1982. "The Bonding Phenomenon: Misinterpretations and Their Implications." *Journal of Pediatrics* 101 (February): 555-557.

Lambert, Wallace E., and Klineberg, Otto. 1967. *Children's Views of Foreign Peoples.* New York: Appleton-Century-Crofts.

Langer, Lawrence. 1991. *Holocaust Testimonies: The Ruins of Memory.* New Haven, CT: Yale University Press.

Lasch, Christopher. 1979. *The Culture of Narcissism.* New York: W. W. Norton.

Laye, Camara. 1975. *Le Regard du Roi.* Paris: Presses Pocket.

Leiderman, P. Herbert. 1981. "Human Mother-Infant Bonding: Is There a Sensitive Phase?" In *Behavioral Development*, eds., Klaus Immelmans, G. W. Barlow, L. Petrinovich, and M. Main. Cambridge, U.K.: Cambridge University Press.

Leith, Emmett. 1995. "Holography." In *The Encyclopedia Americana,* International ed., Vol. 14, 303-307. Danbury, CT: Grolier Inc.

LeVine, Robert A. 1984. "Properties of Culture: An Ethnographic View." In *Culture Theory*, eds. Richard Schweder and Robert LeVine, 67-87. Cambridge, U. K.: Cambridge University Press.

Lewis, Peter H. 1994, September 16. "Persistent E-mail: Electronic Stalking or Innocent Courtship?" *The New York Times,* B-11.

Lewontin, Richard. 2000. *It Ain't Necessarily So.* New York: The New York Review Books.

Lifton, Robert Jay. 1968 *Death in Life.* New York: Random House.

_____. 1976. *The Life of the Self.* New York: Simon and Schuster.

_____. 1987. *The Future of Immortality.* New York: Basic Books.

_____. 1993. *The Protean Self.* New York: Basic Books.

Lomax, Alan. 1968. *Folk Song Style and Culture.* Washington, D.C.: American Association for the Advancement of Science.

Lorenz, Konrad Z. 1952. *King Solomon's Ring.* London: Methuen.

Lovelock, John. 1979. *Gaia.* Oxford, U.K.: Oxford University Press.

Lurigio, Arthur J., Carroll, John S., and Stalans, Loretta J. 1994. "Understanding Judges' Sentencing Decisions: Attributions of Responsibility and Story Construction." In *Applications of Heuristics and Biases to Social Issues,* eds. Linda Heath, R. Scott Tindale, John Edwards, et al., 91-115. New York: Plenum Press.

Lynd, Helen M. 1961. *On Shame and the Search for Identity.* New York: Science Editions.

Mack, John, and Hickler, Holly. 1982. *Vivienne.* New York: New American Library.

Mathabane, Mark. 1987. *Kaffir Boy*. New York: New American Library.

Matson, Floyd. 1966. *The Broken Image*. Garden City, NY: Anchor Books, Doubleday.

Maureille, Bruno. 2002,. "Lost Neanderthal Neonate Found." *Nature* 419 (September 5): 33-34.

May, Rollo. 1981. *Freedom and Destiny*. New York: Delta.

McBride, James. 1997. *The Color of Water*. New York: Riverhead Books.

McTaggert, John M. E. 1922. *Studies in the Hegelian Dialectic*, 2nd ed. Cambridge, U. K.: Cambridge University Press.

Mead, George Herbert. 1964. *On Social Psychology*, ed. Anselm L. Strauss. Chicago: University of Chicago Press.

Mead, Margaret. 1943. *And Keep Your Powder Dry*. New York: William Morrow.

_____. 1954. "The Swaddling Hypothesis: Its Reception." *American Anthropologist* 56 (3): 395-409.

Menard, Louis. 2003, March 24. "The Historical Romance." *The New Yorker*, 78-82.

Mercer, Jane. 1973. *Labeling the Mentally Retarded*. Berkeley, CA: University of California Press.

Merleau-Ponty, Maurice. 1962. *Phenomenology of Perception*. London: Routledge and Kegan Paul.

Merton, Robert K. 1949. *Social Theory and Social Structure*. Glencoe, IL: Free Press.

Middleton, John, ed. 1967. *Myth and Cosmos*. Austin, TX: University of Texas Press.

Miller, Alice. 1983. *The Drama of the Gifted Child*. New York: Basic Books.

Minde, K. 1986. "Bonding and Attachment: Its Relevance for the Present-Day Clinician." *Developmental Medicine and Child Neurology* 28 (December): 803-806.

Montagu, Ashley. 1983. *Growing Young*. New York: Macmillan.

_____. 1998. *Man's Most Dangerous Myth: The Fallacy of Race*, 6th ed. Walnut Creek, CA: AltaMira Press.

Montagu, Ashley, and Matson, Floyd. 1984. *The Dehumanization of Man*. New York: McGraw-Hill.

Montessori, Maria. 1964. *The Montessori Method*. New York: Schocken Books.

_____. 1969. *The Absorbent Mind*. New York: Delta Book, Dell.

Moore, Carol-Lynne. 1987. "Body Metaphors: Some Implications for Movement Education." *Interchange* 18 (No. 3): 31-37.

_____. 1992. "The Body as Dream, the Body as Nightmare." *The Educational Forum* 56 (Summer): 361-370.

_____. 2003. *Introduction to Movement Harmony*. Denver (P.O. Box 11036, Denver, CO 80211): Cottage Industries.

Moore, Carol-Lynne. 2005. *Movement and Making Decisions*. New York: Rosen Publishing Group.

Moore, Carol-Lynne, and Yamamoto, Kaoru. 1988. *Beyond Words*. London: Gordon and Breach.

Mumford, Lewis. 1952. *Art and Technics*. New York: Columbia University Press.

_____. 1967. *Technics and Human Development*. New York: Harcourt Brace Jovanovich.

Mure, G. R. G. 1950. *A Study of Hegel's Logic*. Oxford, U.K: Oxford University Press.

Murphy, Robert F. 1990. *The Body Silent*. New York: W. W. Norton.

Murray, D. W. 1993. "What Is the Western Concept of the Self? On Forgetting David Hume." *Ethos* 21 (1): 3-23.

Myers, Barbara. 1984. "Mother-Infant Bonding: The Status of the Critical Period Hypothesis." *Developmental Review* 4 (September): 240-274.

Myrdahl, Gunnar. 1969. *Objectivity in Social Research*. New York: Pantheon Books.

Neill, A. S. 1960. *Summerhill*. New York: Hart.

Ortega y Gasset, José. 1962. *History as a System*. New York: W. W. Norton.

Oyler, Chris. 1988. *Go toward the Light*. New York: Harper and Row.

Panofsky, Erwin. 1940. *The Codex Huygens and Leonardo da Vinci's Art Theory*. London: Warburg Institute.

Parks, Gordon. 1986. *Choice of Weapons*. St. Paul: Minnesota Historical Society.

Payer, Lynn. 1989. *Medicine and Culture*. Hammondsworth, Middlesex, England: Penguin Books.

Peale, Norman Vincent. 1952. *The Power of Positive Thinking*. Englewood Cliffs, NJ: Prentice-Hall.

Pepper, Stephen C. 1942. *World Hypothesis*. Berkeley, CA: University of California Press.

Piaget, Jean. 1976. *To Understand Is to Invent*. Hammondsworth, Middlesex, England: Penguin Books.

Polanyi, Michael. 1962. *Personal Knowledge*. Chicago: University of Chicago Press.

_____. 1967. *The Tacit Dimension*. Garden City, New York: Anchor Books.

Porte, Alain. 1992. *François Delsarte: Une Anthologie*. Paris: Édition IPMC.

Postman, Neil. 1993. *Technopoly*. New York: Vintage Books.

Pribram, Karl H. 1971. *Languages of the Brain*. Englewood Cliffs, NJ: Prentice-Hall.

Rank, Otto. 1978. *Will Therapy*. New York: W. W. Norton.

Reinsmith, William A. 1989. "The Whole in Every Part: Steiner and Waldorf Schooling." *The Educational Forum* 54 (Fall): 79-91.

Ricoeur, Paul. 1992. *Oneself as Another.* Chicago: University of Chicago Press.

Rieff, David. 1991. "Victims, All?" *Harper's Magazine* (October): 49-56.

Riesman, David. 1967. "Some Questions about the Study of American Character in the Twentieth Century." *Annals of the American Academy of Political and Social Science* 370 (March): 36-47.

Riley, Gresham. 1980. "The Reform of General Education." *Liberal Education* 66 (Fall): 299.

Rogers, Carl R. 1961. *On Becoming a Person.* Boston: Houghton Mifflin.

Rokeach, Milton. 1960. *The Open and Closed Mind.* New York: Basic Books.

Rosenberg, Morris. 1965. *Society and the Adolescent Self-Image.* Princeton, NJ: Princeton University Press.

_____. 1989. *Society and the Adolescent Self-Image*, rev. ed. Middleton, CT: Wesleyan University Press.

Rosenberg, Morris, and Simmons, Roberta. 1972. *Black and White Self-Esteem.* Washington, D.C.: American Sociological Association.

Rosenberger, Nancy R., ed. 1994. *Japanese Sense of Self.* Cambridge, U. K.: Cambridge University Press.

Rosenthal, Robert, and Jacobson, Lenore. 1989. *Pygmalion in the Classroom.* New York: Irvington.

Rothenberg, David. 1993. *Hand's End.* Berkeley, CA: University of California Press.

Rucker, Rudolf v.B. 1977. *Geometry, Relativity and the Fourth Dimension.* New York: Dover.

Rybczynski, Witold. 1987. *Home.* New York: Viking.

Sachs, Peter. 1996. *Generation X Goes to College.* Chicago: Open Court.

Saint-Exupéry, Antoine de. 1948. *Citadelle.* Paris: Edition Gallimard.

Sandburg, Carl. 1960. *Harvest Poems: 1910-1960.* New York: Harcourt, Brace and World.

Sanford, Anthony J. 1987. *The Mind of Man.*

Sarton, May. 1973. *Journal of a Solitude.* New York: W. W. Norton.

_____. 1981. *The House by the Sea.* New York: W. W. Norton.

_____. 1987. *At Seventy.* New York: W. W. Norton.

Scheff, Thomas J. 1999. *Being Mentally Ill*, 3rd ed. New York: Aldine.

Schimmel, Solomon. 1997. *The Seven Deadly Sins.* Oxford, U.K.: Oxford University Press.

Schofield, Carey, and Smith, Michael. 2000. "New US Missiles Will Destroy Our Past, Says Russia." *The Daily Telegraph* (London, December 5), xx.

Schwartz, Steven. 1994. "Heuristics and Biases in Medical Judgment and Decision Making." In *Applications of Heuristics and Biases to Social Issues*, eds. Linda Heath, R. Scott Tindale, John Edwards, et al., 45-72. New York: Plenum Press.

Scott-Maxwell, Florida. 1979. *The Measure of My Days.* New York: Penguin Books.

Sedlak, Michael, et al. 1986. *Selling Students Short*. New York: Teachers College Press.

Seligman, Martin E. P. 1998, July. "The American Way of Blame." From the *APA Monitor* 29 (7) [www.apa.org/monitor], 2pp.

Shelley, Mary. [1881] 1981. *Frankenstein*. New York: Bantam Books.

Shore, Bradd. 1996. *Culture in Mind*. New York: Oxford University Press.

Shweder, Richard, and LeVine, Robert, eds. 1984. *Culture Theory*. Cambridge, U. K.: Cambridge University Press.

Simonton, O. Carl, Matthews-Simonton, Stephanie, and Creighton, James L. 1978. *Getting Well Again*. New York: Bantam Books.

Smith, Frank. 1990. *To Think*. New York: Teachers College Press.

Snow, C. P. 1959. *The Two Cultures and the Scientific Revolution*. Cambridge, U. K.: Cambridge University Press.

Sorokin, Pitirim A. 1956. *Fads and Foibles in Modern Sociology and Related Sciences*. Chicago: Henry Regnery.

Spiegel, David. 1997. "Hypnosis and Suggestion." In *Memory Distortion*, ed. Daniel L. Schacter, 129-149. Cambridge, MA:: Harvard University Press.

Steinberg, Laurence. 1996. *Beyond the Classroom*. New York: Simon and Schuster.

Stravinsky, Igor. 1970. *Poetics of Music*. Cambridge, MA: Harvard University Press.

Sullivan, Harry Stack. 1953. *The Interpersonal Theory of Psychiatry*. New York: W. W. Norton.

Sutcliffe, Anthony J. 1985. *On the Track of Ice Age Mammals*. Cambridge, MA: Harvard University Press.

Suzuki, D. T. 1961. *Essays in Zen Buddhism (First Series)*. New York: Grove Press.

_____. 1974. "Lectures on Zen Buddhism." In *Zen Buddhism and Psychoanalysis,* by Erich Fromm, D. T. Suzuki, and Richard De Martino, 1-76. London: Souvenir Press.

Tavris, Carol. 1993. "Beware the Incest-Survivor Machine." *The New York Times Book Review* (January 3): 1 & 16-17.

Taylor, Shelley E. 1989. *Positive Illusions*. New York: Basic Books.

Terkel, Studs, ed. 1996. *Coming of Age*. New York: St. Martin's Press.

Thornton, Yvonne S. 1996. *The Ditchdigger's Daughters*. New York: New American Library.

Tillich, Paul. 1952. *The Courage to Be*. New Haven, CT: Yale University Press.

Toepfer, Karl. 1998. *Empire of Ecstasy*. Berkeley, CA: University of California Press.

Tocqueville, Alexis de. [1835] 1991. *Democracy in America*, vol. 2. New York: Alfred A. Knopf.

Toth, Susan Allen. 1987. "The Importance of Being Remembered." *The New York Times Book Review* (June 28): 1+.

Toulmin, Stephen. 1982. *The Return to Cosmology*. Berkeley, CA: University of California Press.

Trevelyan, George. 1990. "Preface." In *The New Holistic Herbal*, 3rd ed., by David Hoffmann, 5. London: Element Books.

Truitt, Anne. 1984. *Daybook*. New York: Penguin Books.

_____. 1997. *Prospect*. New York: Penguin Books.

United Nations. 1989. *Convention on the Right of the Child*. New York: Author.

Wallace, William. [1892] 1959. *The Logic of Hegel*, 2nd ed., revised and augmented. Oxford, U.K.: Oxford University Press. [Translated from the first part of Hegel's *The Encyclopaedia of the Philosophical Sciences*, 1817.]

Weatherall, David. 2002, January 27. "The Professor: We Understand Very Little." *The Sunday Times* (London). Section 5: 2.

Weltner, Linda. 1990. *No Place like Home*. Boston: William Morrow.

Wharton, Edith. 1919. *French Ways and Their Meaning*. New York: D. Appleton.

Wheelis, Allen. 1959. *The Quest for Identity*. New York: W. W. Norton.

White, Tim D., Asfaw, Berhane, Degusta, et al. 2003. "Pleistocene *Homo sapiens* from Middle Awash, Ethiopia." *Nature* 423 (June 12): 742-747.

White, Tim D., Suwa, Gen, and Asfaw, Berhane. 1994 "*Australopithecus ramidus*, a new species of early hominid from Aramis, Ethiopia." *Nature* 371 (September 22): 306-312.

White, William H. 1970. *The Last Landscape*. Garden City, NY: Doubleday.

Wiesel, Elie. 1997, September 13-19. "Le Passé Évoque l'Abîme." *France-Amérique* (San Francisco), 28.

Wigginton, Eliot. 1986. *Sometimes a Shining Moment*. Garden City, NY: Anchor Press/Doubleday.

Wilson, Edward O. 1978. *On Human Nature*. Cambridge, MA: Harvard University Press.

Wilson, Frank R. 1998. *The Hand*. New York: Pantheon Books.

Winnicott, D. W. 1988. *Babies and Their Mothers*. Reading, MA: Addison-Wesley.

Wolpoff, Milford H., Senut, Brigitte, Pickford, Martin, and Hawks, John. 2002. "*Sahelanthropus* or '*Sahelpithecus*'?" *Nature* 419 (October 10): 581-582.

Yamamoto, Kaoru. 1975. *Individuality*. Columbus, OH: Charles E. Merrill.

_____. 1988. "To See Life Grow: The Meaning of Mentorship." *Theory into Practice* 27 (Summer): 183-189.

_____. 1993. *Their World, Our World*. Westport, CT: Praeger.

Yeats, William Butler. 1950. "A Prayer for Old Age." In *The Collected Poems of W. B. Yeats*. London: Macmillan. [Originally in *A Full Moon in March*. (1935).]

Young, Leontine. 1966. *Life among the Giants*. New York: McGraw-Hill.
————. 1971. *Wednesday's Children*. New York: McGraw-Hill.
Young-Bruehl, Elizabeth. 1996. *Anatomy of Prejudices*. Cambridge, MA: Harvard University Press.
Zollikofer, Christoph P. E., Ponce de Léon, et al. 2005. "Virtual Cranial Reconstruction of *Sahelanthropus tchadensis*." *Nature* (April 7): 755-759.

Index

About the Author

Kaoru Yamamoto is Professor Emeritus of Educational Psychology at the University of Colorado, and Fellow of the American Psychological Association. Educated at the University of Tokyo (B.S. in Engineering) and the University of Minnesota (M.A. and Ph.D.), he had taught at Kent (Ohio) State University, University of Iowa, Pennsylvania State University, and Arizona State University (Distinguished Teacher Award) before moving to Colorado.

He also guest taught at the University of Washington, Simon Fraser University (Canada), University of Victoria (Canada; Landsdowne Scholar), University of Iceland (Fulbright Scholar), Zheziang Provincial University (China; Project Specialist, U.N. International Development Bank), and Azusa Pacific University (Center Scholar, the Center for the Study of Ethics and Values).

In addition to six scores of journal articles and several book chapters, his previous publications include *The College Student and His Culture* ; *Teaching* ; *The Child and His Image*; *Individuality* ; *Death in the Life of Children*; *Children in Time and Space*; *Beyond Words* (with Carol-Lynne Moore); *Their World, Our World*; and *Children and Stress* (with Beverly Hardcastle Stanford). He also served as the editor of the *American Educational Research Journal* and the *Educational Forum*.